HUMAN RESOURCES

Volume III

Talent Management in the

Digital Age

Develop high-impact business strategies

HUMAN RESOURCES
Volume III Talent Management in the Digital Age ©
Series: Human Resources
Deluxe Edition – Soft Cover

Written, illustrated and edited by:
Marbella Yeniree Moya Ochoa

Copyright © 2023
First edition ISBN: 9798866290925
Independent editions
Caracas Venezuela

General Content

DEDICATION

To God and the Blessed Virgin.
To my mother and father Xiomara and Pedro.
To my sisters Mara and Linda.
To my beloved Valeria, Samuel, Santiago,
Miguel, Mateo and my Alfrides Miguel.
My eternal love with you.

FOREWORD

Digital transformation has changed the way companies operate and manage their human resources. The role of human resources professionals in the digital age is more critical than ever, as they must face new challenges and opportunities to attract, develop and retain talent.

In this book, we will explore emerging trends and practices in human talent management in the digital age.

From using artificial intelligence and data analytics to creating meaningful work experiences and building inclusive, multigenerational company cultures, we will examine how companies are responding to the challenges and seizing opportunities of the digital age to foster success and long-term growth in an increasingly competitive economy.

It is with great excitement that I present to you my third book in the Human Resources series.

Thank you so much for reading me!
THE AUTHOR

INTRODUCTION

In the digital age, human talent management has become a vital issue for the success of companies. Here digital transformation has changed the way organizations search, attract, retain and develop their staff.

Today, human resources management must adapt to new technologies, tools and trends in order to attract and retain the best talent.

Personnel selection, training, evaluation, communication and motivation processes has a significant impact on human talent management.

The ability to effectively manage human talent is essential for the company's competitiveness and long-term success.

In this context, human resources leaders must be aware of the latest trends and talent management tools in order to stay ahead and cope with market demands.

HUMAN RESOURCES

Volume III
Talent Management in the
Digital Age

CHAPTER I
Talent Management

Talent management is a process that involves identifying, developing and retaining an organization's most talented personnel. It includes activities such as candidate selection and recruitment, training and skills development, performance appraisal, and succession planning. The ultimate goal is to ensure that the organization has the right talent to achieve its long-term goals.

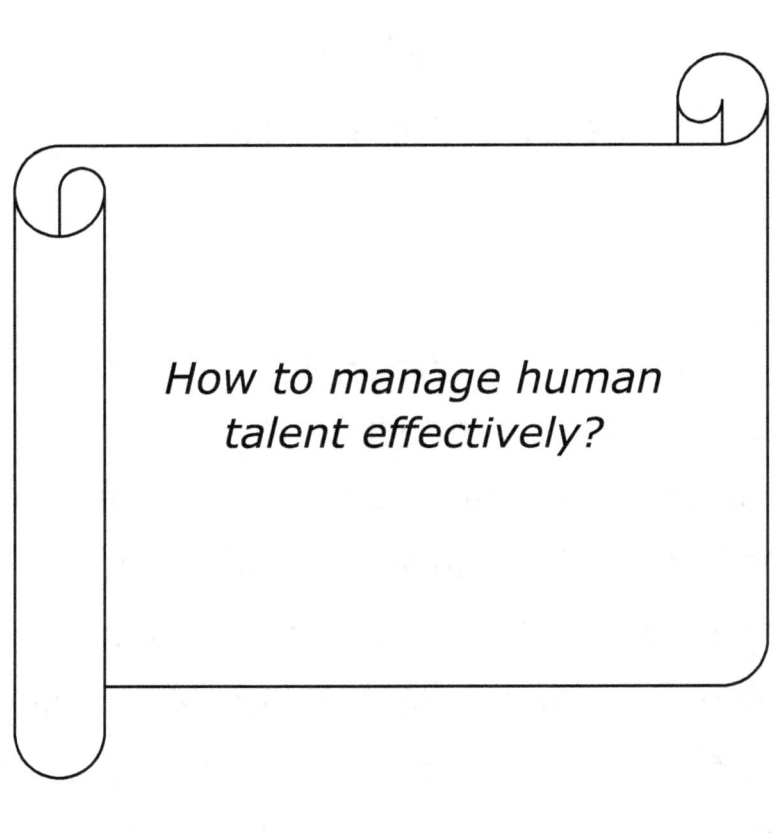

How to manage human
talent effectively?

A key aspect of talent management is identifying the employees with the greatest potential within the organization. This is achieved through performance assessment and skills analysis, as well as direct observation of the employee's behavior and competencies. Once these employees are identified, they can be provided with training and skill development to help them reach their full potential and further contribute to the success of the organization.

Human talent management focuses on attracting, selecting, developing and retaining the right personnel to achieve the company's objectives. It includes human resources planning , performance evaluation, skills development and work environment management.

Teamwork is important because it allows you to combine different skills and perspectives to achieve common goals. Collective intelligence can also arise from a team that knows how to use its skills and resources effectively.

One way to improve teamwork is to set clear goals and communicate them to the entire team. It is also important to assign specific tasks to each member and ensure that everyone has the necessary resources to complete them. Finally, fostering a culture of collaboration and open communication can help build a more united and efficient team.

Talent management refers to a set of practices and processes designed to attract, develop and retain the best employees in an organization. This includes activities such as succession planning, training and development, and performance appraisal.

***

Mind Map No. 1

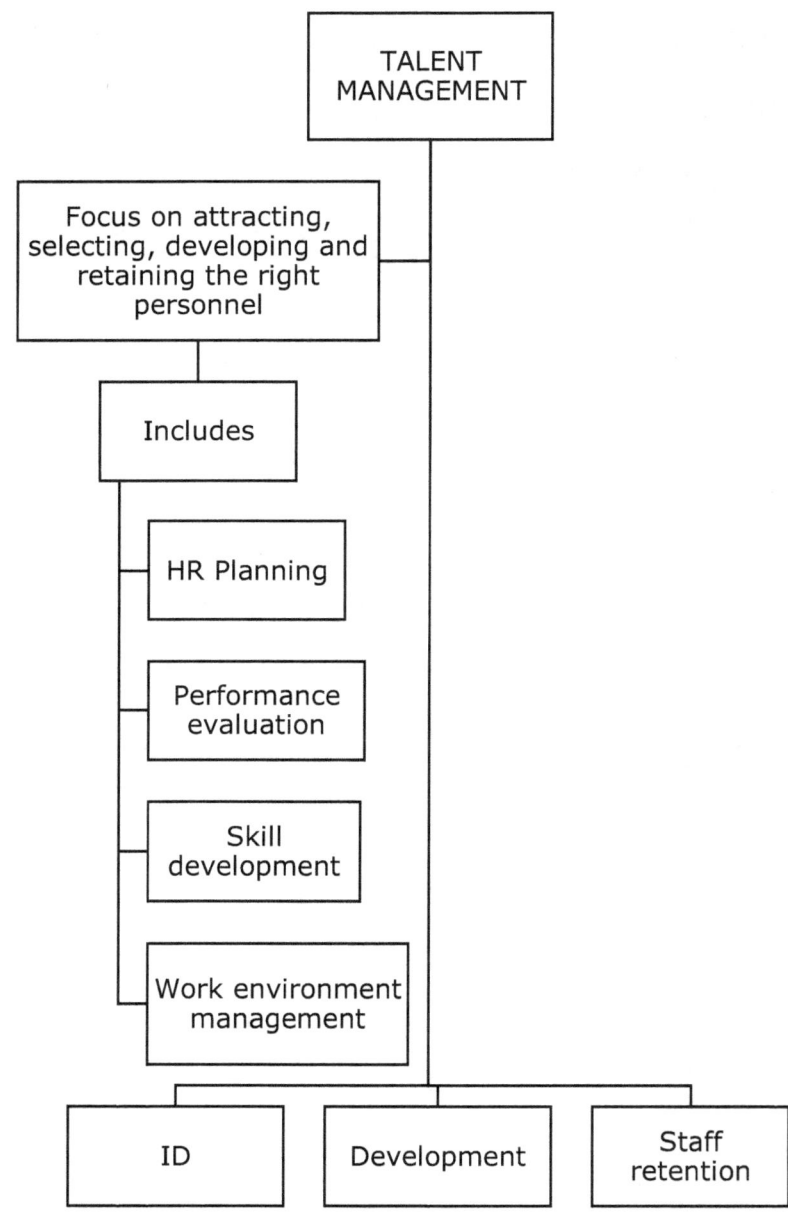

TALENT MANAGEMENT

Focus on attracting, selecting, developing and retaining the right personnel

Includes

HR Planning

Performance evaluation

Skill development

Work environment management

ID

Development

Staff retention

Your Mind Map No. 1

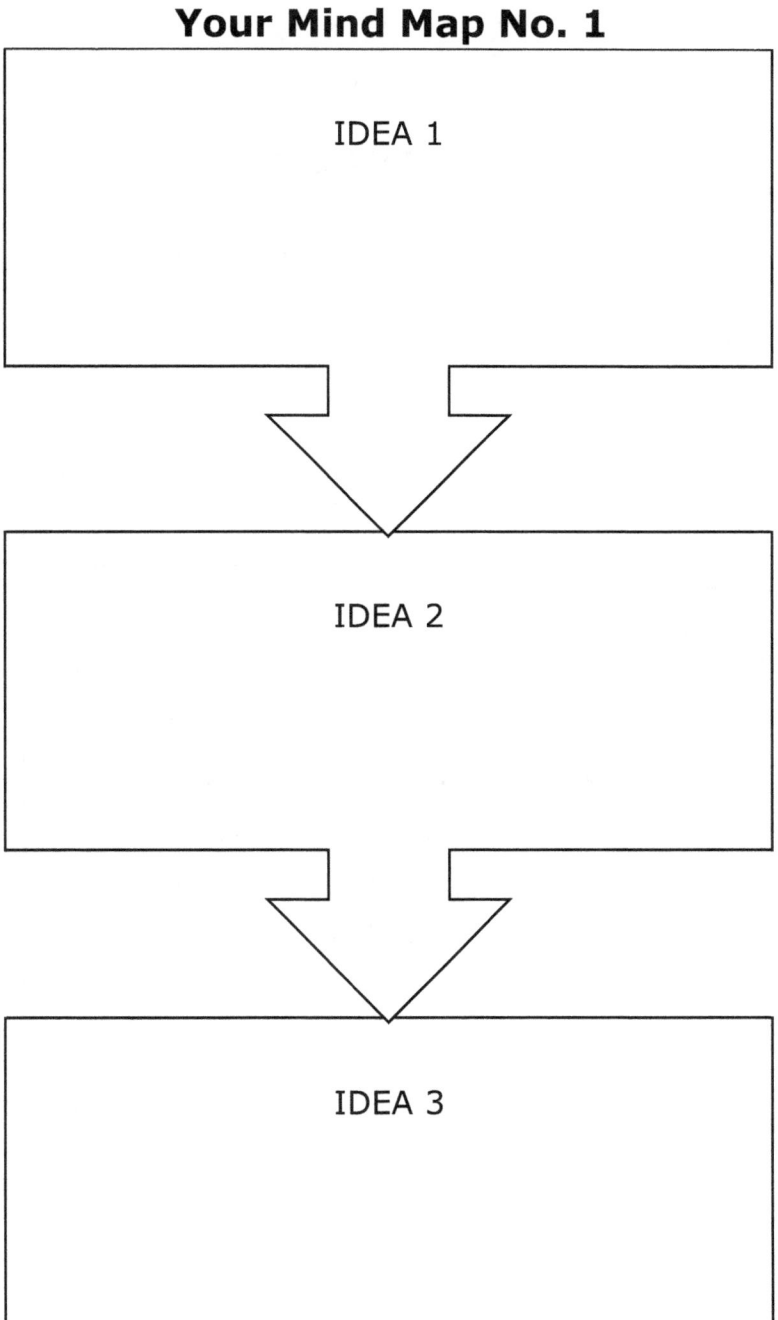

CHAPTER II

Attract and Retain

How can a company attract and retain the most talented employees in a highly competitive market?

In addition to what I've already mentioned, there are a few other strategies that can help attract and retain the most talented employees:

1. Have a clear mission and values.

Talented employees want to work for companies that have a clear purpose and are committed to ethical and responsible values.

2. Offer opportunities for learning and growth.

Talented employees want to be constantly learning and developing, so offering training and mentoring programs can be very attractive.

3. Promote diversity and inclusion.

Companies that value diversity and inclusion are more likely to attract and retain talented employees, as this allows them to work in a more innovative, creative and collaborative environment.

4. Offer a flexible work environment.

Talented employees value flexibility in their work schedules, as well as the ability to work from home or remotely.

5. Recognize a job well done.

Talented employees want to feel valued and recognized for their work, so offering incentives and recognition can be a good strategy to retain them.

Mind Map No. 2

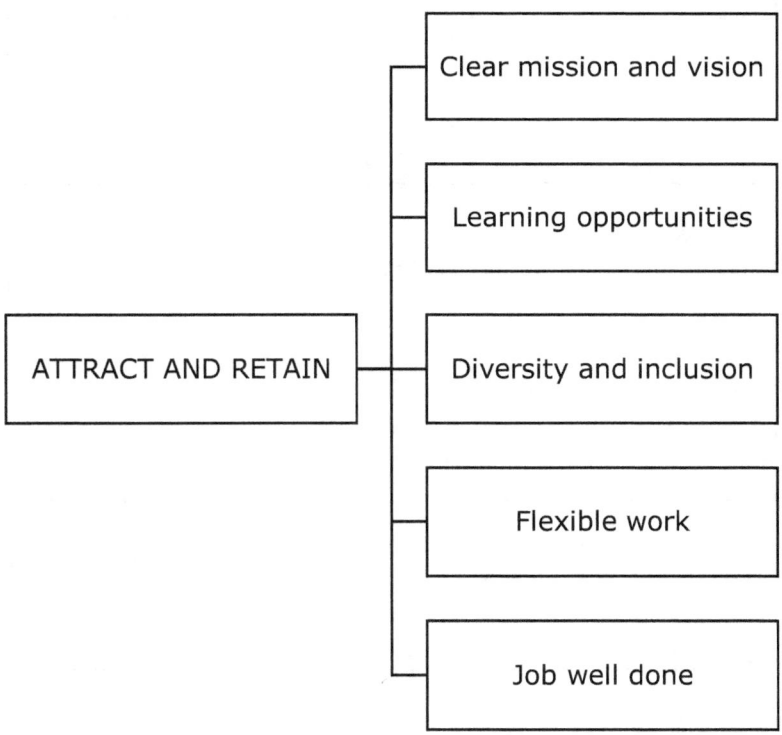

Your Mind Map No. 2

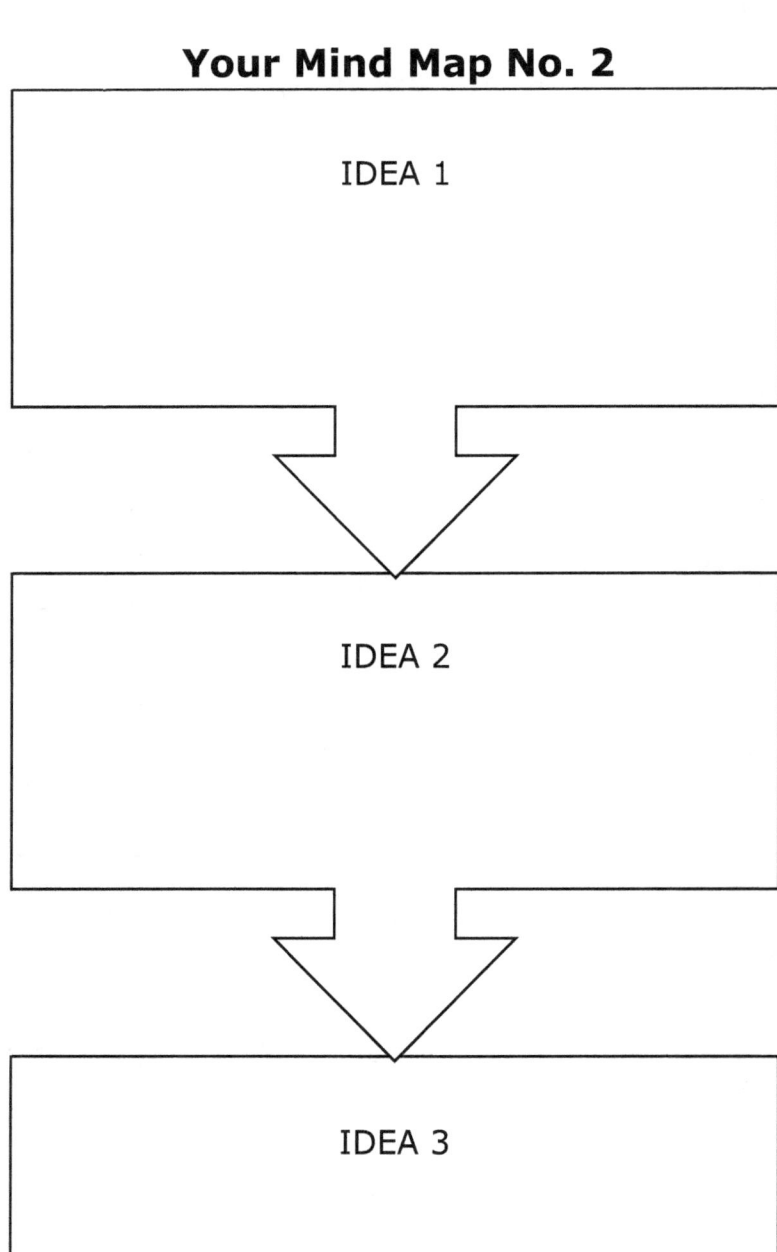

CHAPTER III

Identification and Retention

How can a company develop an effective mentoring program to help retain and develop talent?

Identifying and retaining talent is key to the success of any company.

Some effective strategies include creating career plans, promoting professional development, fair and competitive compensation, and recognizing and rewarding exceptional performance.

***

Mind Map No. 3

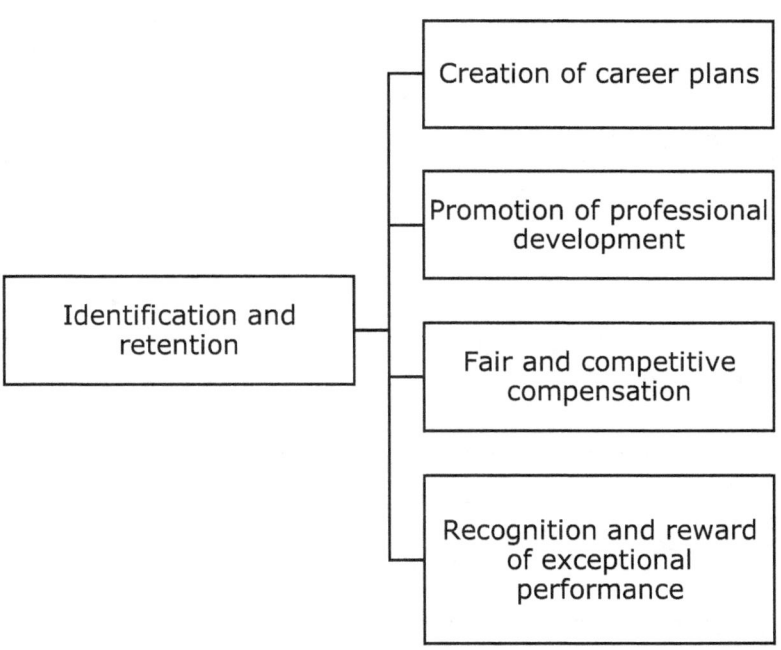

Your Mind Map No. 3

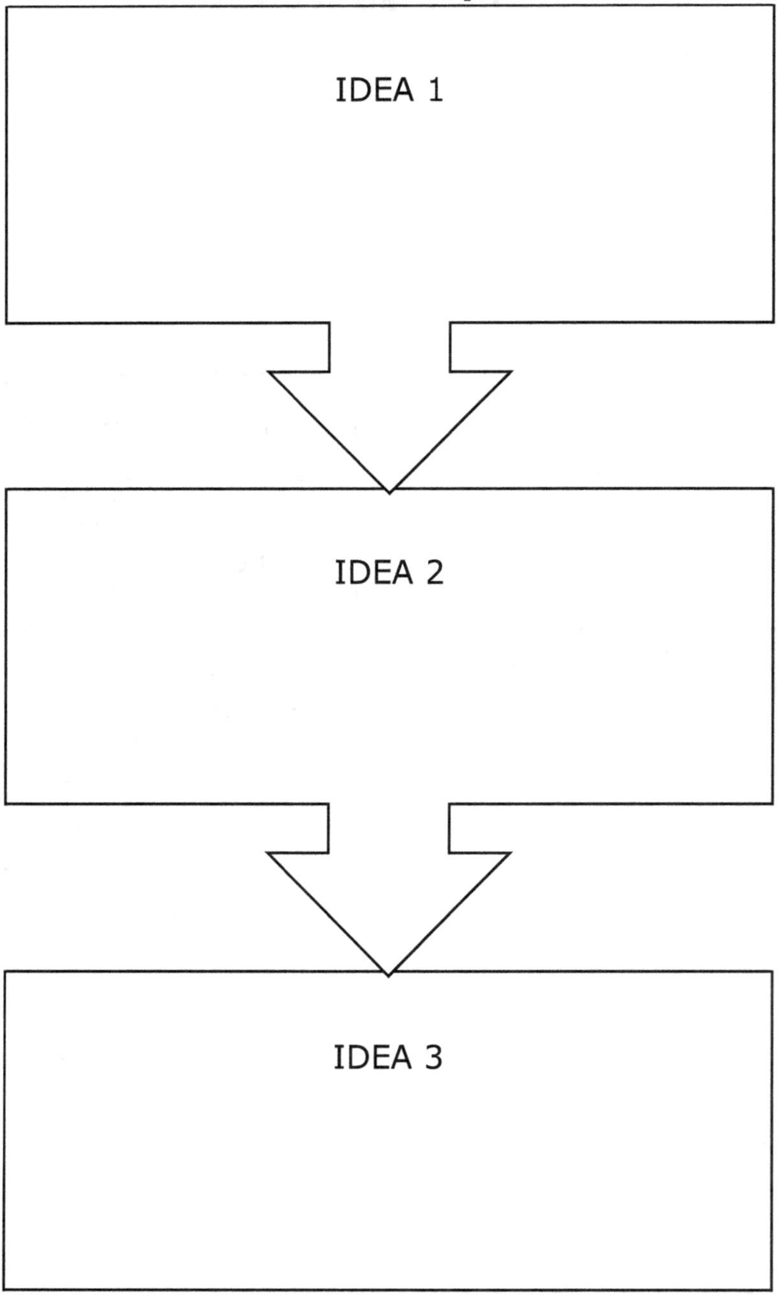

IDEA 1

IDEA 2

IDEA 3

CHAPTER IV
Succession Planning

Succession planning refers to the identification and development of employees with the potential to take on key roles within an organization in the future. This involves assessing the skills and competencies needed for each position and working to develop employees so they are ready to take on those responsibilities when necessary.

How can a company ensure it is identifying and preparing the right employees to take on key roles in the future as current leaders retire or move on to other roles?

To implement effective succession planning, it is important to consider the following steps:

✓ Identify the key positions and the skills necessary for each of them.

✓ Assess current employees to identify those with the potential to take on those roles in the future.

✓ Create individualized development plans for each of these employees, providing them with the necessary opportunities and resources to acquire the necessary skills.

✓ Establish an ongoing monitoring and evaluation process to ensure employees are progressing appropriately and adjust the development plan as necessary.

Succession planning is a long-term investment in the organization, as it ensures continuity of leadership and long-term business success.

***

Mind Map No. 4

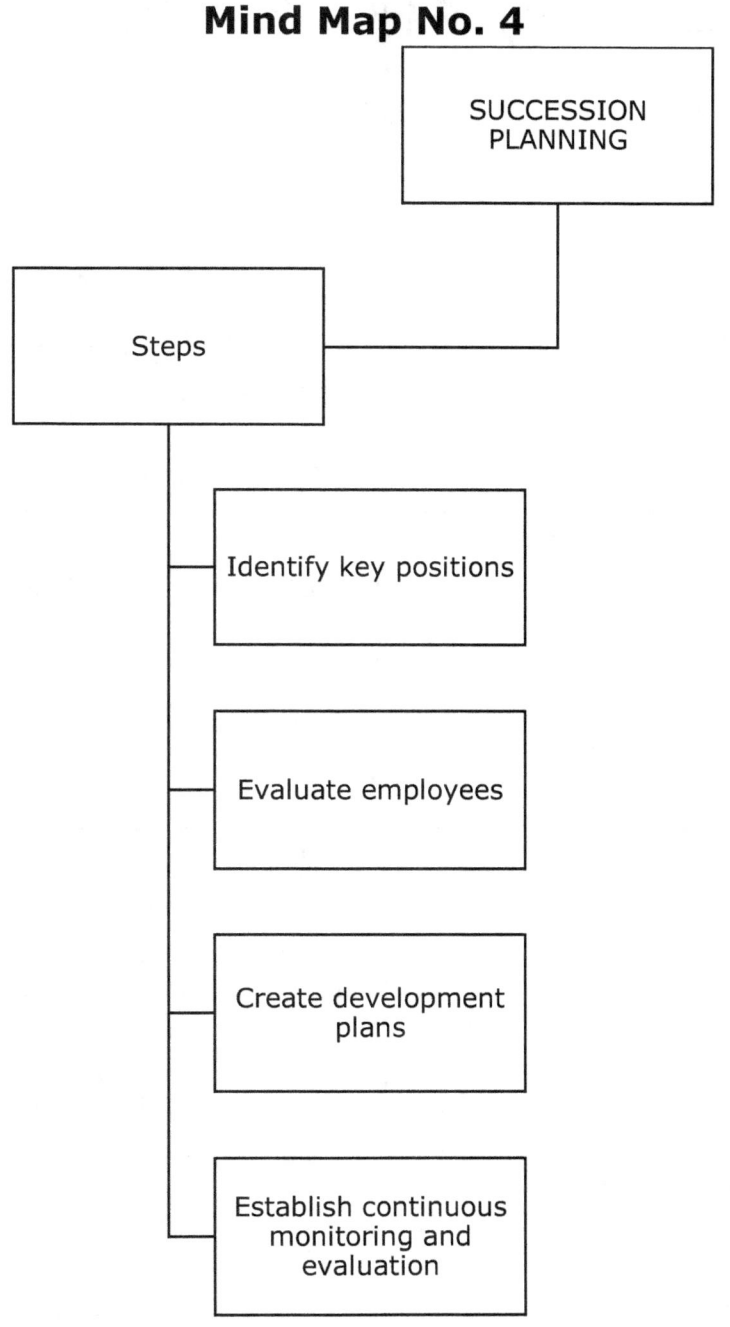

SUCCESSION PLANNING

Steps

Identify key positions

Evaluate employees

Create development plans

Establish continuous monitoring and evaluation

Your Mind Map No. 4

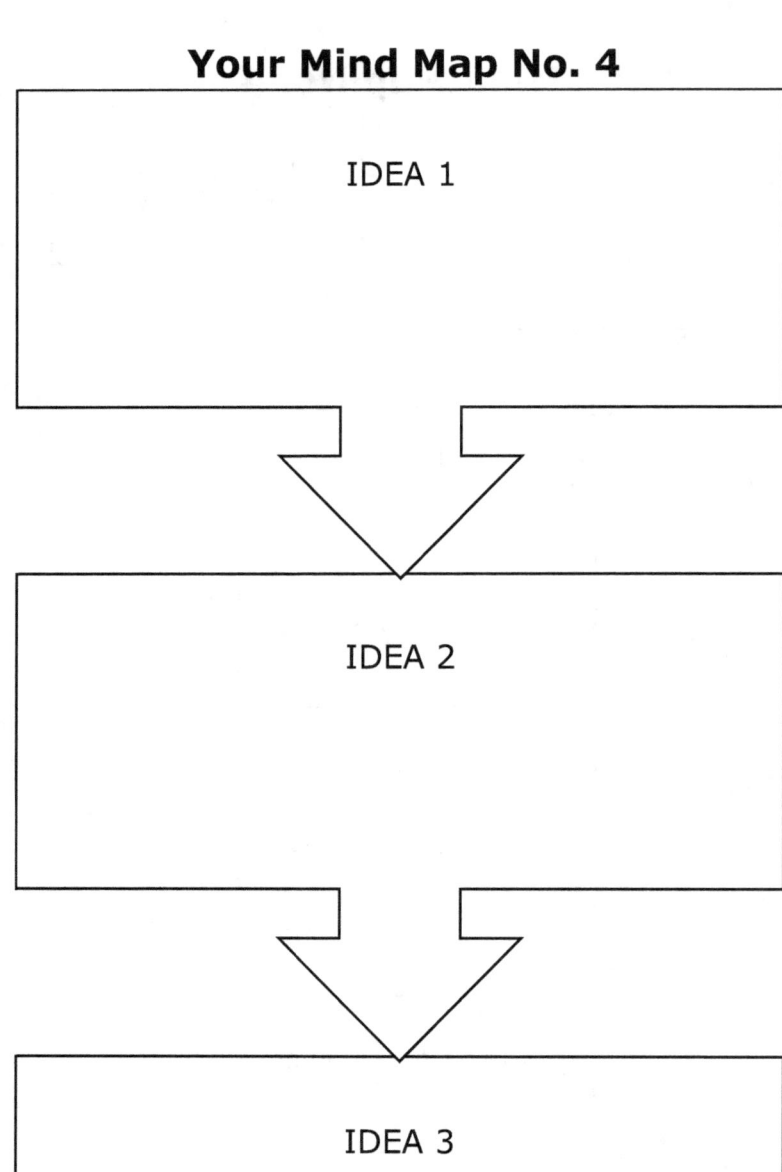

CHAPTER V
Creation of Career Plans

Career plans are a set of objectives, skills and experiences that are planned over the long term to help employees achieve their career goals within an organization.

These plans include identifying development opportunities, defining clear objectives, and tracking progress toward those goals.

How can a company ensure that its career plans are inclusive and equitable for all employees, regardless of gender, race or socioeconomic background?

Career plans are a tool that helps you define your long-term professional goals and the steps necessary to achieve them. To create a career plan, it is important to identify your strengths, weaknesses, and areas of interest.

Next, you should set clear and realistic goals to advance your career and seek development opportunities that will allow you to acquire the skills necessary to achieve those goals. It is also important to consider opportunities for growth and promotion within your organization or in the job market.

A well-designed career plan will help you advance your career effectively and achieve your long-term career goals.

To create a career plan, it is important to start by defining your long-term professional goals.

Then, identify the skills and experiences necessary to achieve those goals and look for development opportunities that will allow you to acquire those skills and experiences. It's also important to establish an action plan with specific goals and realistic deadlines to measure your progress.

Don't hesitate to seek advice and guidance from your organization's leaders or an experienced mentor to help you create and achieve your career goals.

***

Mind Map No. 5

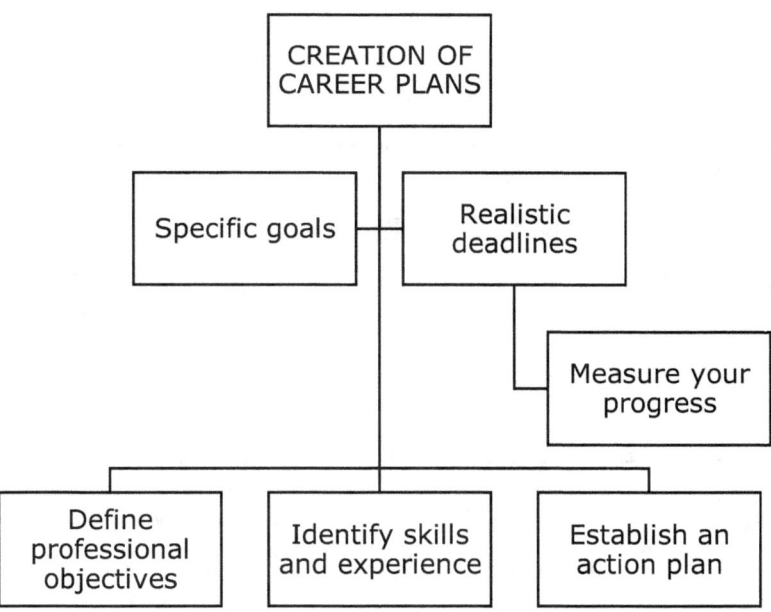

Your Mind Map No. 5

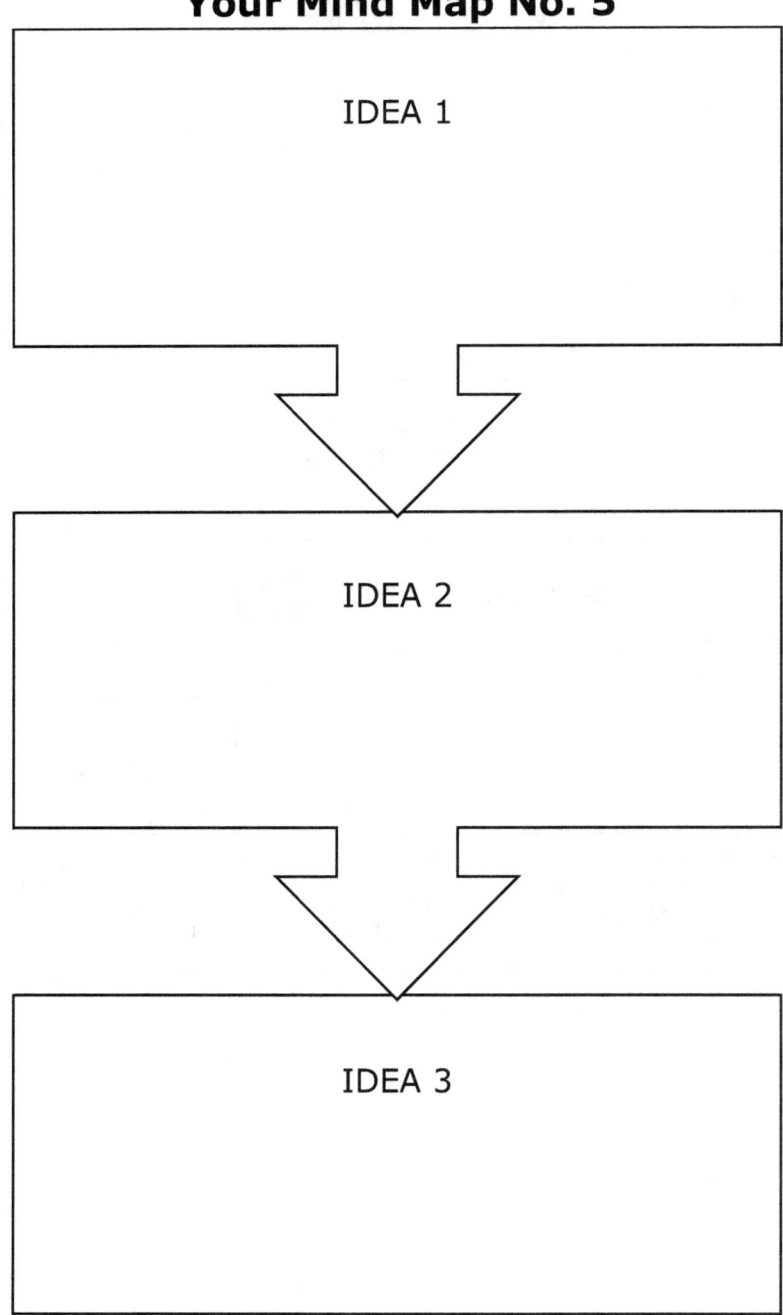

CHAPTER VI

Exercise to Create a Career Plan

Why is it important for employees to follow the exercises and tasks assigned in a career plan to achieve their professional and personal goals?

- ✓ A good exercise for creating a career plan is to write a list of your long-term career goals, such as occupying a management position in your company or becoming an expert in a certain area.
- ✓ Then, make a list of the skills and experiences needed to achieve those goals.
- ✓ Next, identify the development opportunities available in your organization or in the market that allow you to acquire those skills and experiences.
- ✓ Finally, establish an action plan with specific goals and realistic deadlines to measure your progress toward your goals. Remember that it is important to be flexible and adjust your plan

based on your changing needs and circumstances.

***

Mind Map No. 6

Your Mind Map No. 6

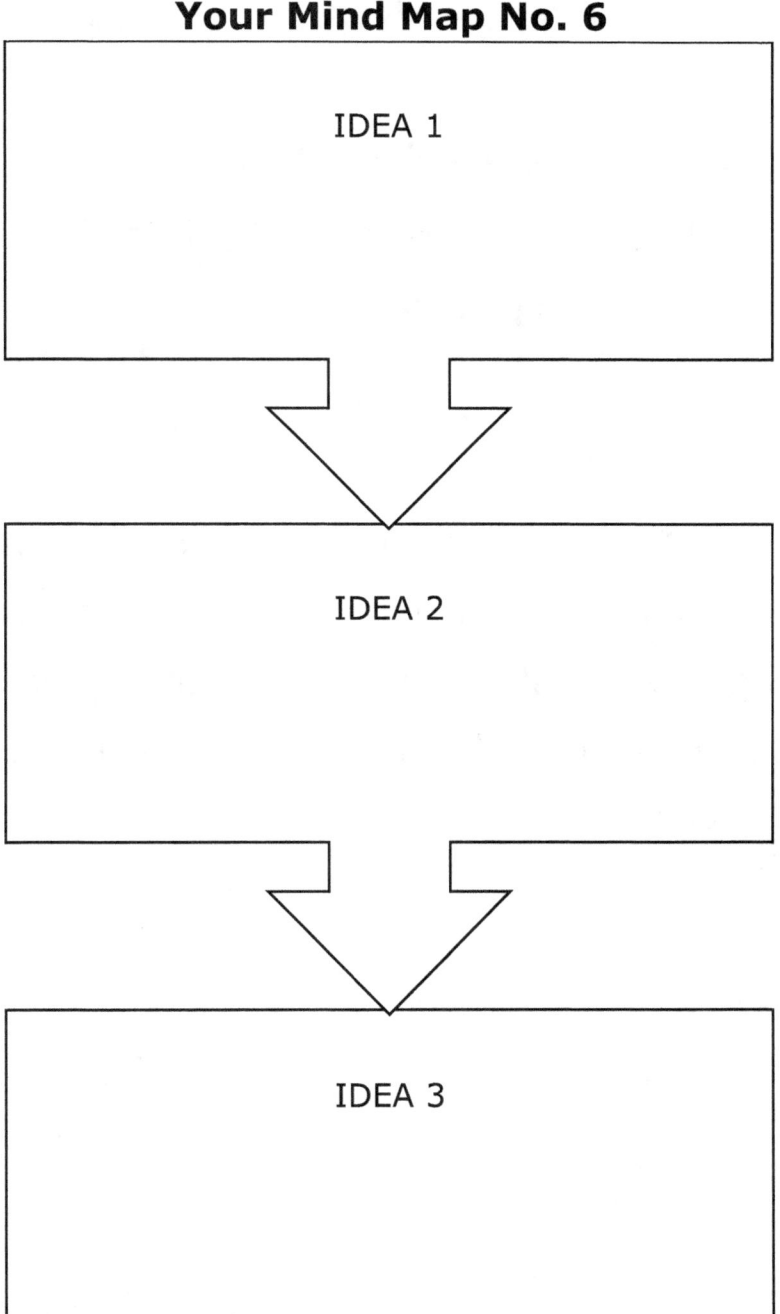

CHAPTER VII
Promotion of Professional Development

The promotion of professional development is a continuous process of improving skills and knowledge that takes place throughout the working career.

What steps can a company take to promote the professional development of its employees and encourage their growth within the organization?

This advancement may include acquiring new skills, earning certifications, participating in training and development programs, and seeking growth opportunities on the job.

Promoting professional development may also include identifying and tracking clear goals for career advancement, as well as actively seeking opportunities to learn and grow professionally.

***

Mind Map No. 7

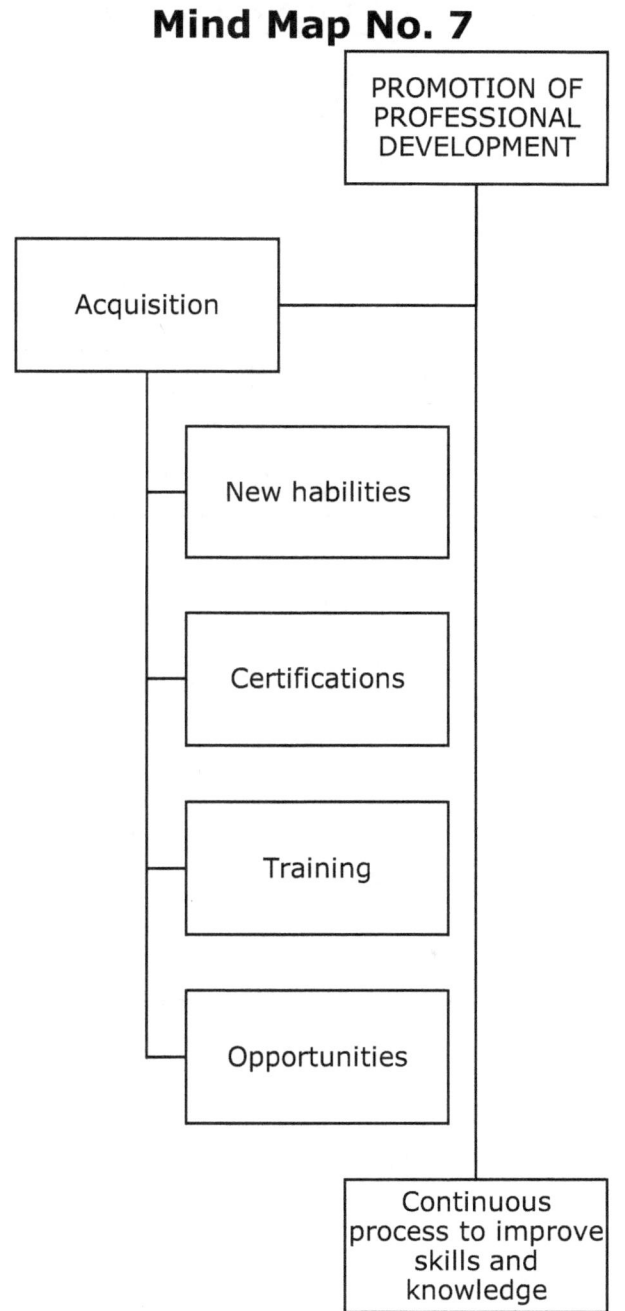

Your Mind Map No. 7

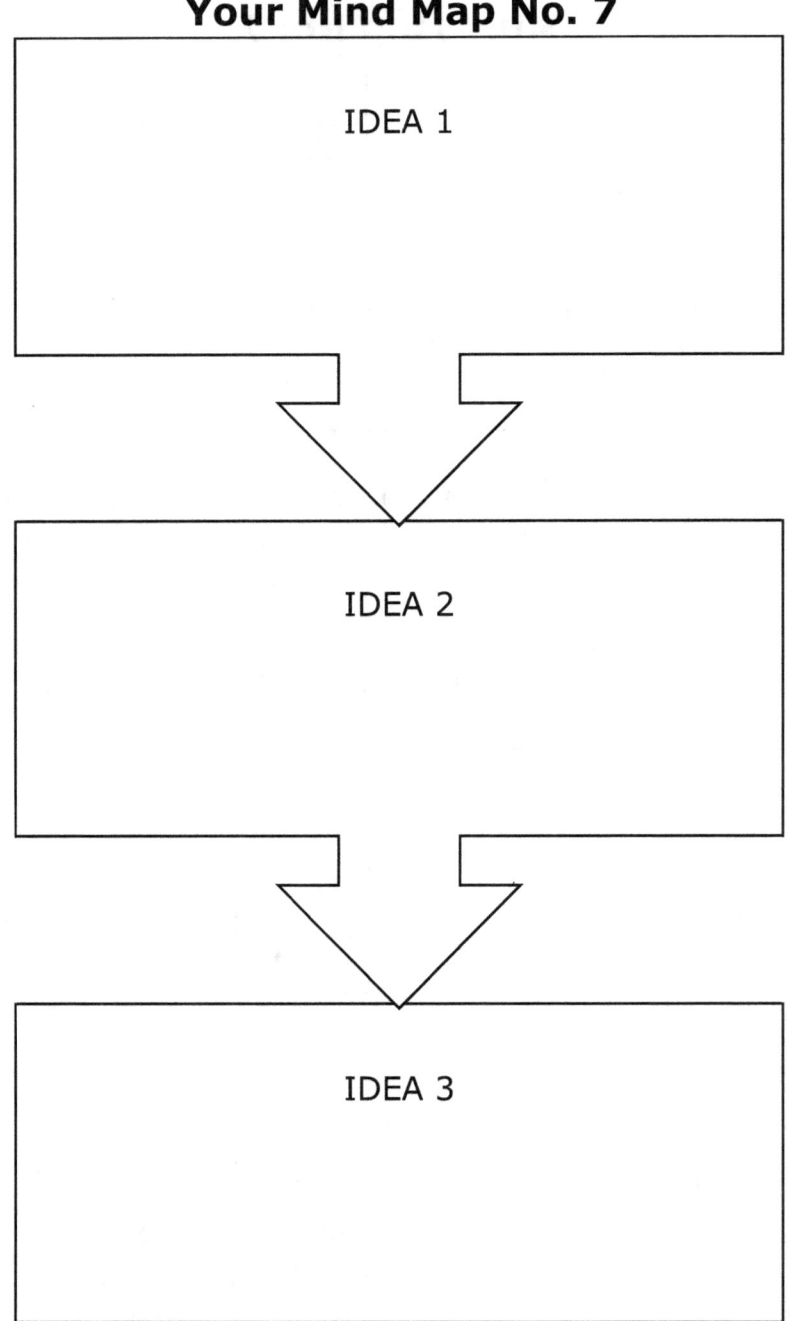

CHAPTER VIII
Professional Development
Promotion Exercise

How can career development exercises help employees improve their skills and knowledge, and stay current in their field of work?

- ✓ A good exercise to promote professional development is to identify your professional strengths and weaknesses.
- ✓ You can make a list of skills, knowledge and experiences that you already have, as well as those that you need to improve or acquire.
- ✓ Next, establish an action plan with specific goals and realistic deadlines to improve your skills and knowledge in the areas you need to develop.
- ✓ Look for training and development opportunities in your organization or in the market that allow you to acquire those skills and experiences.
- ✓ It may also be helpful to seek guidance and support from an experienced mentor or career coach to help you

achieve your career development goals.

***

Mind Map No. 8

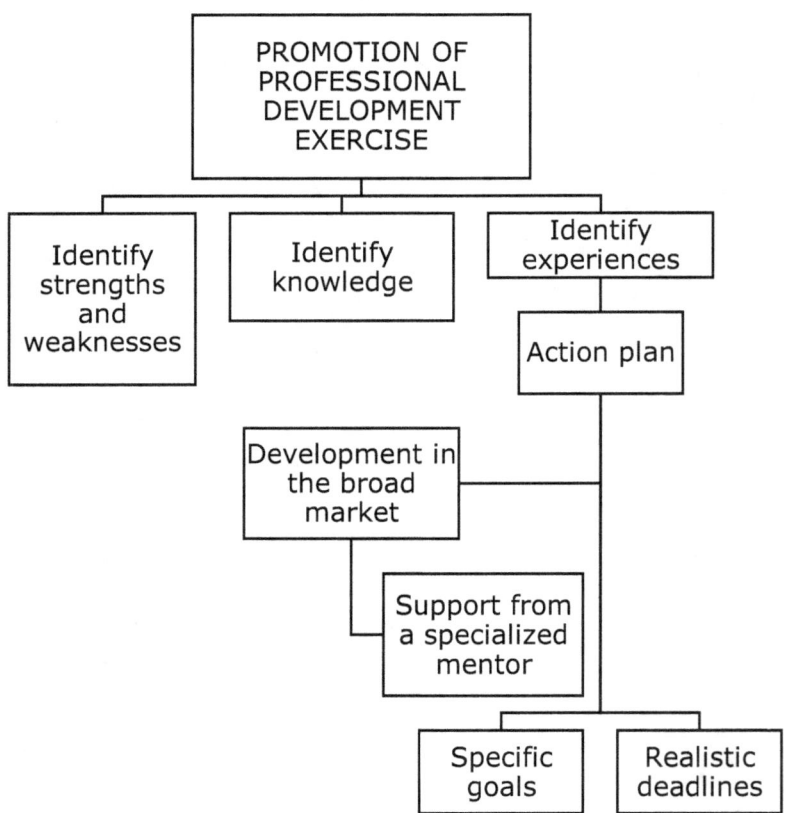

Your Mind Map No. 8

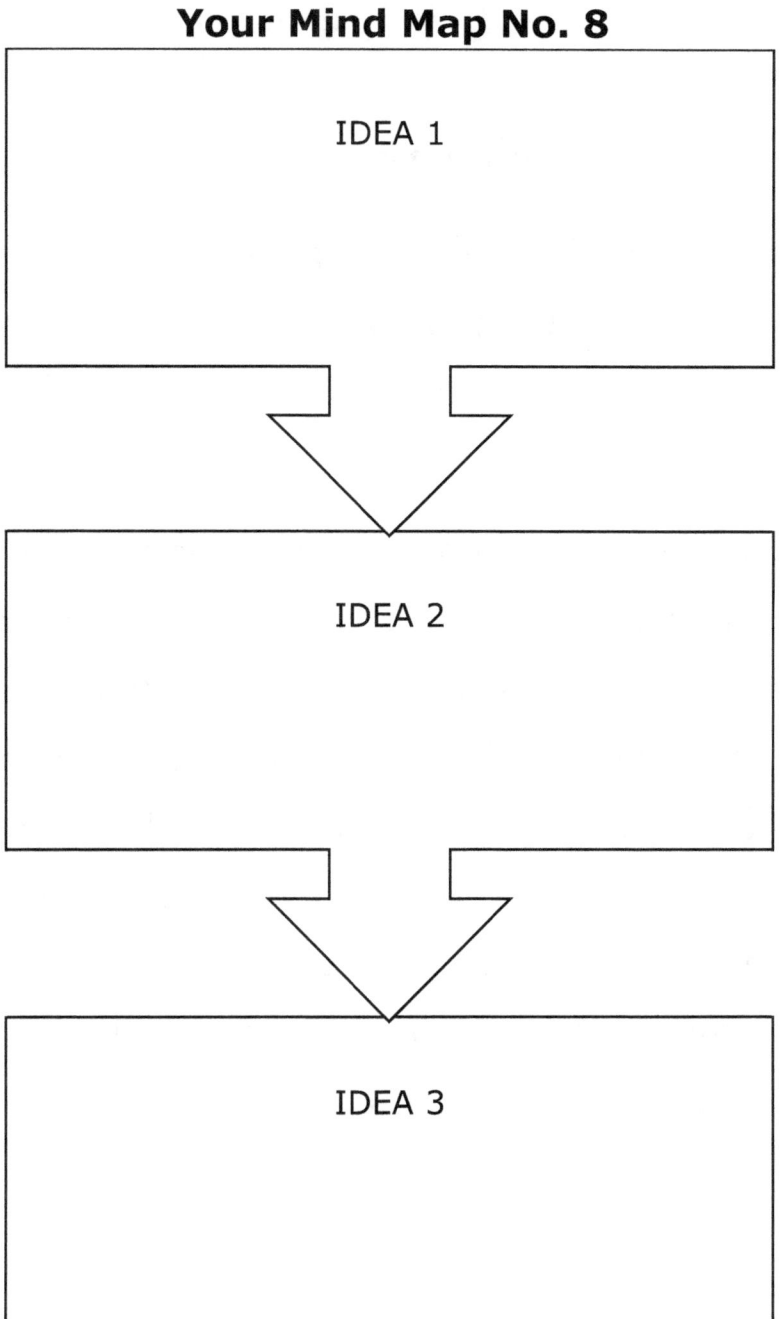

CHAPTER IX
Fair and Competitive Compensation

Fair and competitive compensation is a compensation approach that seeks to provide employees with fair and equitable pay compared to other employees in the same position or similar roles in the labor market. This approach is based on the idea that employees should be compensated fairly for their work and contribution to the organization.

What is your opinion on the importance of offering fair and competitive compensation to attract and retain top talent in an organization?

To achieve fair and competitive compensation, companies often conduct market research to determine the salaries and benefits offered by other similar organizations.

They may also use performance-based compensation systems, where employees are rewarded for exceptional performance through pay increases, bonuses, or additional incentives.

***

Mind Map No. 9

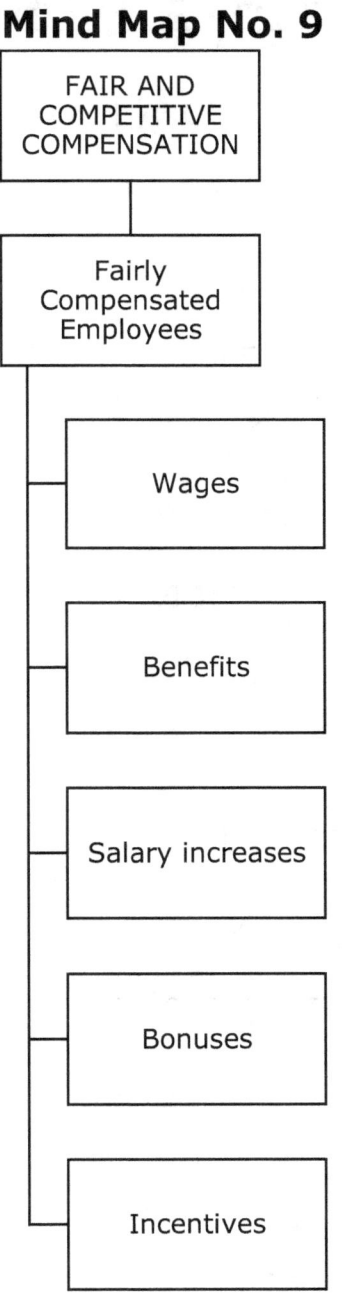

FAIR AND COMPETITIVE COMPENSATION

Fairly Compensated Employees

Wages

Benefits

Salary increases

Bonuses

Incentives

Your Mind Map No. 9

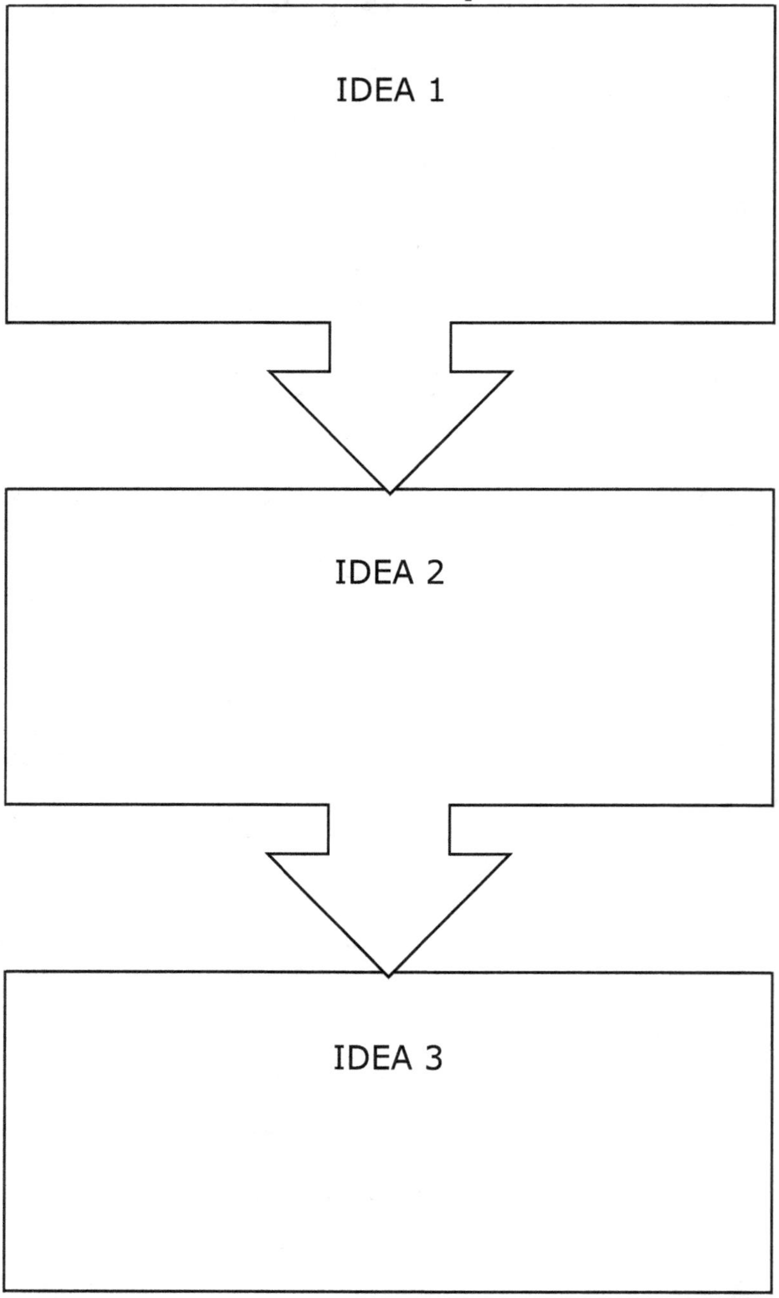

IDEA 1

IDEA 2

IDEA 3

CHAPTER X

Exercise on Fair and Competitive Compensation in Talent Management

A good exercise to ensure that compensation is fair and competitive is to conduct market research to compare salaries and benefits offered by other companies in the same industry and geographic location, and adjust employee compensation accordingly.

Why is it important for a company to have a fair and competitive compensation plan to retain its most talented employees and attract new talent at the same time?

A fair and competitive compensation practice is to conduct regular labor market assessments to ensure that the salaries and benefits offered are competitive, and also take into account factors such as experience, performance, and contribution to the company's success when establishing the salaries of employees.

In addition to the practices mentioned, it is important to establish a clear salary and benefit structure that is based on the job description and the skill and experience requirements necessary to perform the job.

It is also advisable to offer incentives and bonuses for exceptional performance and provide career development and growth opportunities to retain valuable talent.

Mind Map No. 10

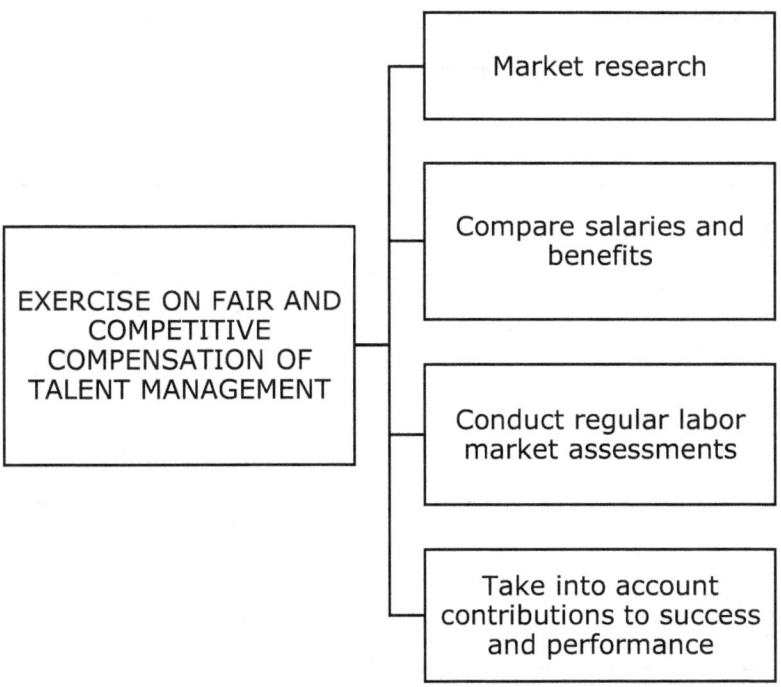

EXERCISE ON FAIR AND COMPETITIVE COMPENSATION OF TALENT MANAGEMENT

- Market research
- Compare salaries and benefits
- Conduct regular labor market assessments
- Take into account contributions to success and performance

Your Mind Map No. 10

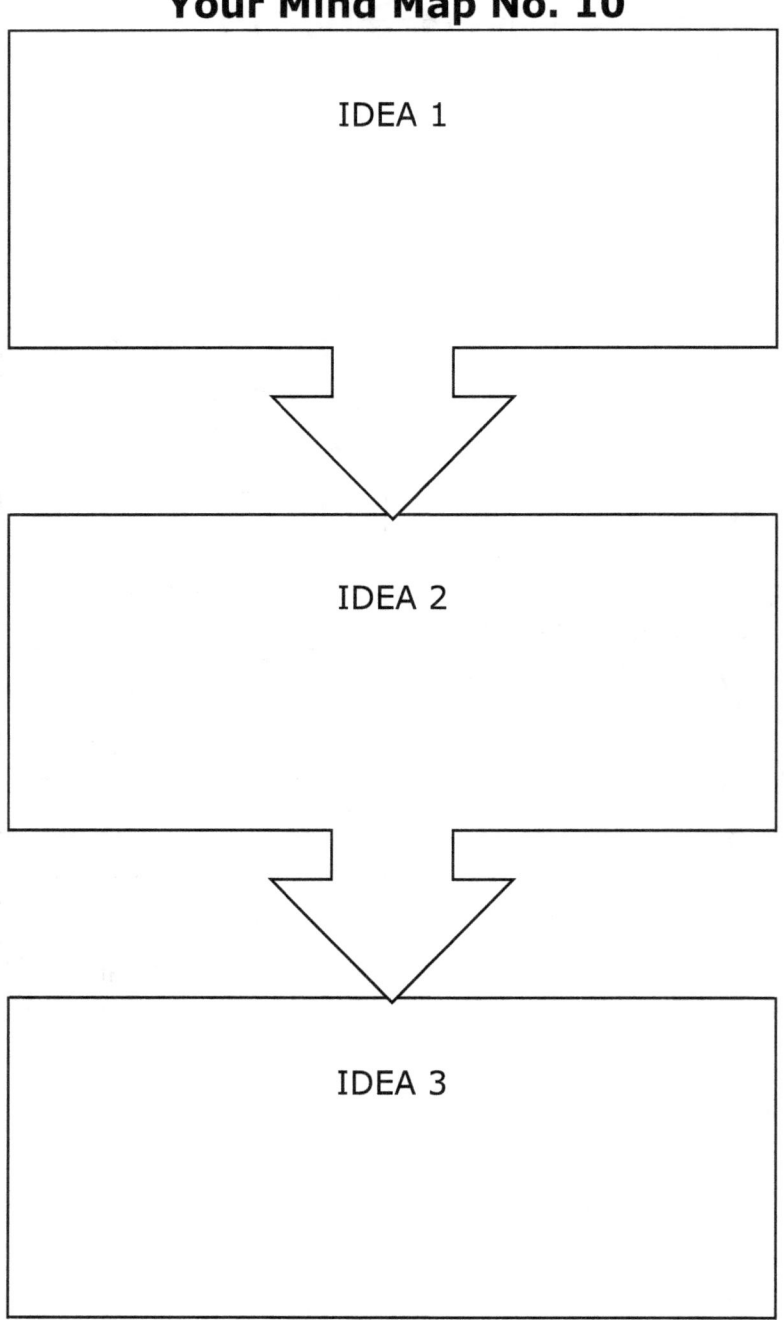

IDEA 1

IDEA 2

IDEA 3

CHAPTER XI

Recognition and Rewarding Exceptional Performance in Talent Management

Recognizing and rewarding exceptional performance is critical to motivating and retaining talented employees. This can include anything from a simple verbal thank you to cash prizes, promotions, and professional development opportunities.

Is there recognition of your performance in your organization?

It is important that recognition is timely, specific and meaningful to the employee, and that it is linked to company objectives and organizational values.

***

Mind Map No. 11

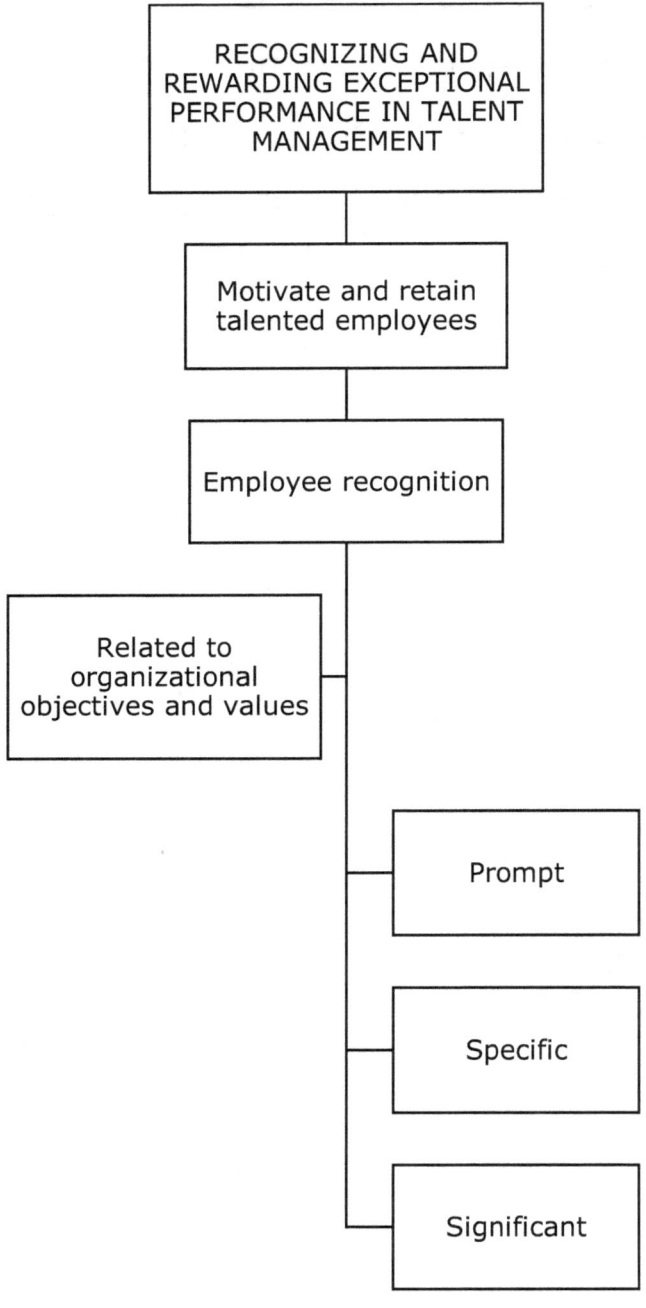

RECOGNIZING AND REWARDING EXCEPTIONAL PERFORMANCE IN TALENT MANAGEMENT

Motivate and retain talented employees

Employee recognition

Related to organizational objectives and values

Prompt

Specific

Significant

Your Mind Map No. 11

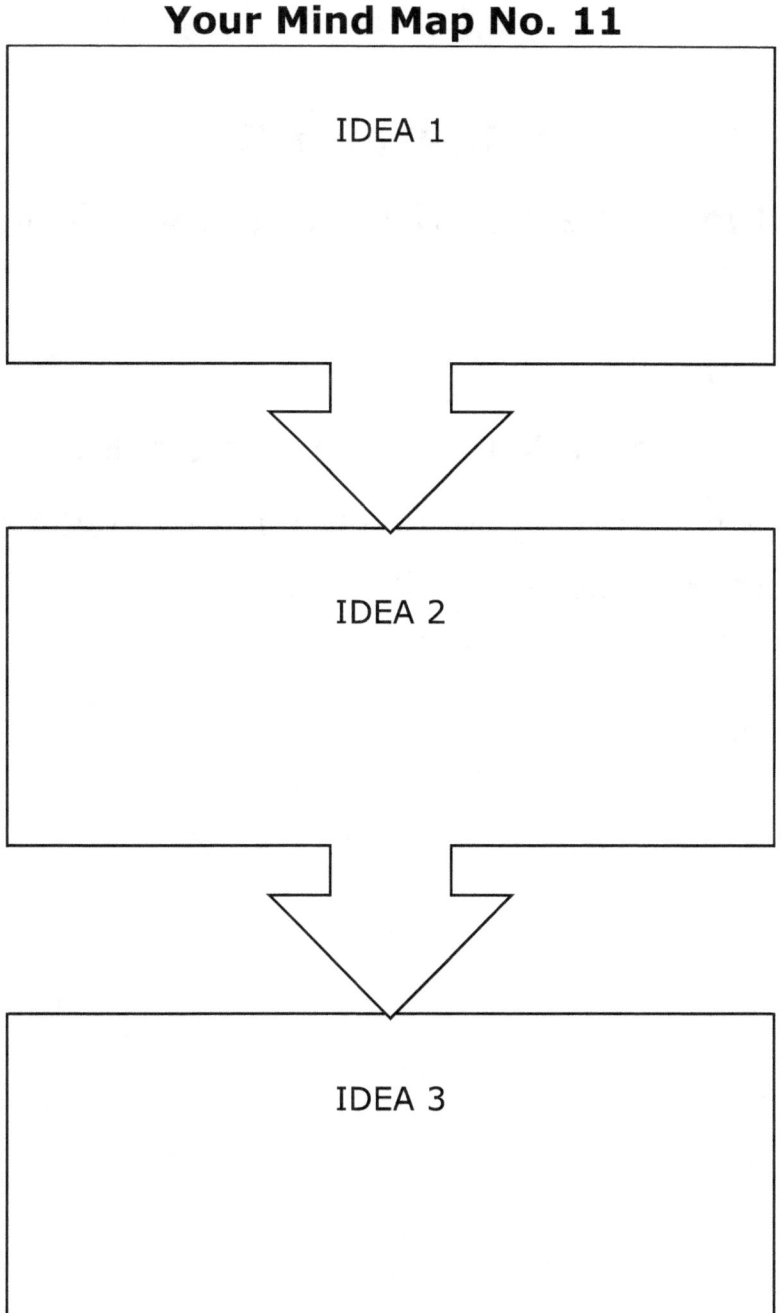

IDEA 1

IDEA 2

IDEA 3

CHAPTER XII
Motivate and Retain Employees

Motivating and retaining employees is essential to maintaining an engaged and productive workforce.

How motivated do you feel in your work?

Some effective practices to motivate and retain employees include:

✓ Offer professional development and training opportunities.
✓ Provide regular and constructive feedback on performance.
✓ Offer a safe, comfortable and healthy work environment.
✓ Provide fair and competitive compensation and benefits.
✓ Promote a healthy work-life balance.
✓ Recognize and reward exceptional performance.
✓ Foster a culture of collaboration, inclusion and diversity.

***

Mind Map No. 12

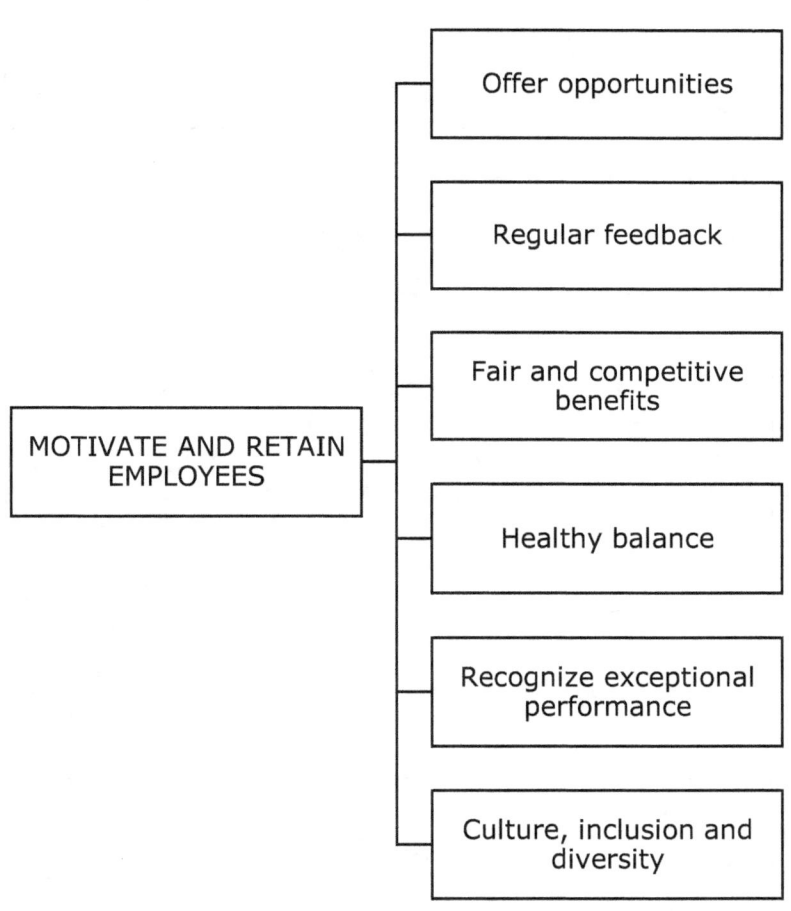

MOTIVATE AND RETAIN EMPLOYEES

- Offer opportunities
- Regular feedback
- Fair and competitive benefits
- Healthy balance
- Recognize exceptional performance
- Culture, inclusion and diversity

Your Mind Map No. 12

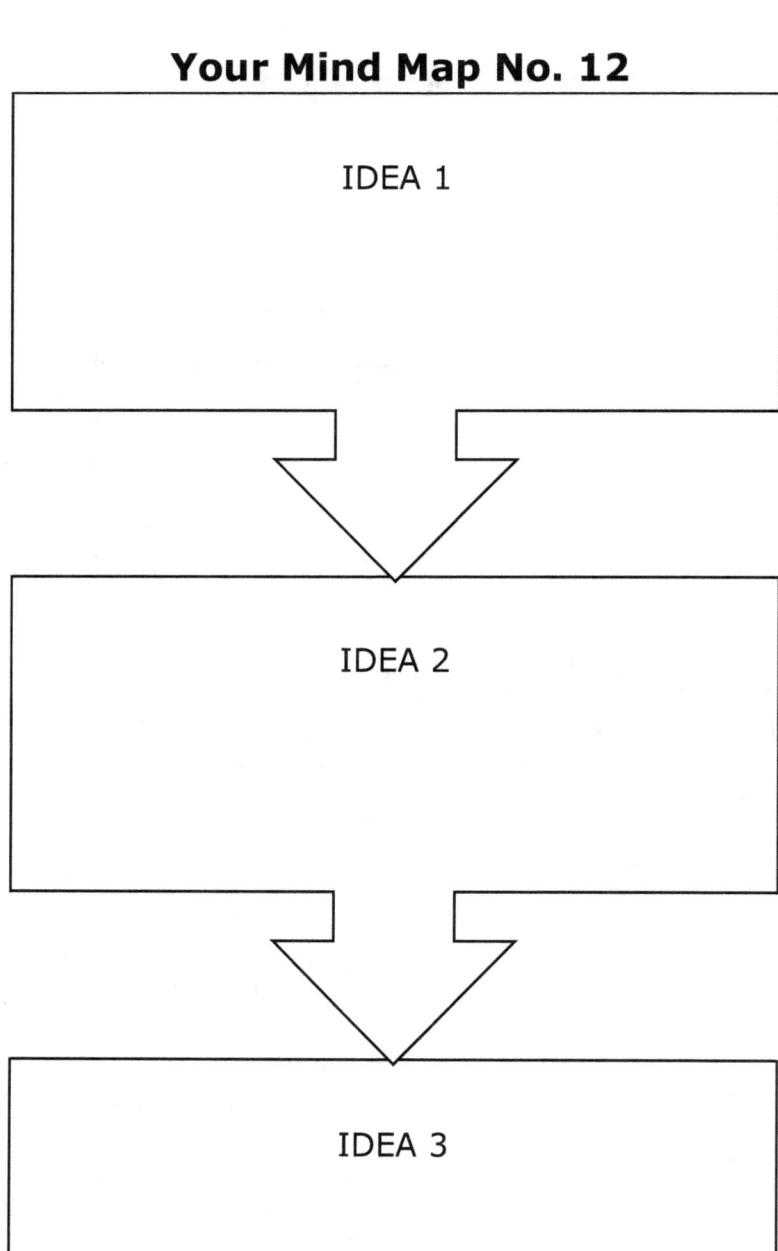

IDEA 1

IDEA 2

IDEA 3

CHAPTER XIII

Exercise on Recognition

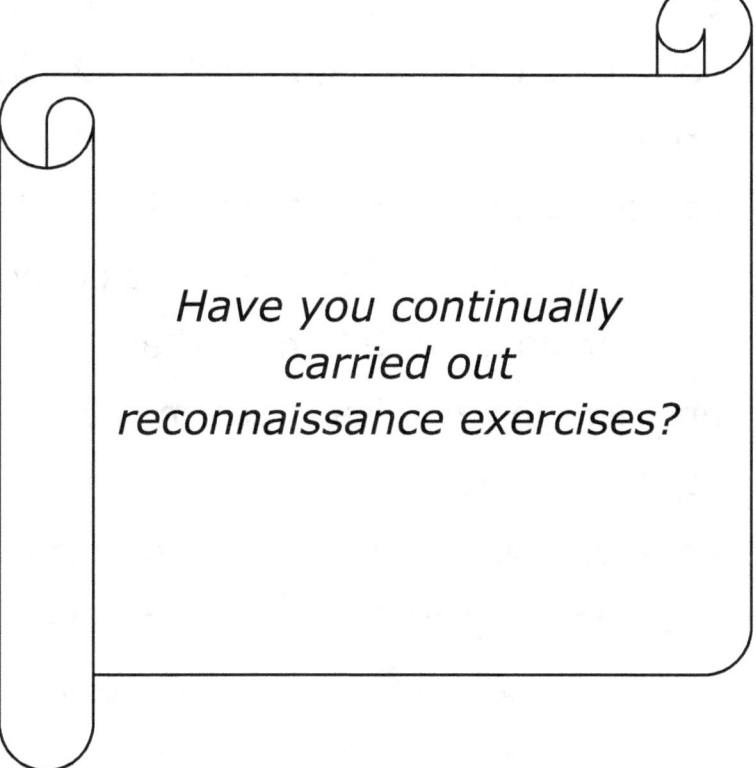

Have you continually carried out reconnaissance exercises?

- ✓ An exercise in recognition could be to establish an "employee of the month" program in which an exceptional employee is recognized and rewarded each month.
- ✓ Recognition could include a photo on the wall of outstanding employees, a certificate of recognition and/or a cash prize.
- ✓ For the program to be effective, it is important that the criteria for selecting the "employee of the month" are clear and fair, and are clearly communicated to all employees.
- ✓ Additionally, it is important to ensure that the program is not biased toward any specific department or position and that both individual and team contributions are recognized.

***

Mind Map No. 13

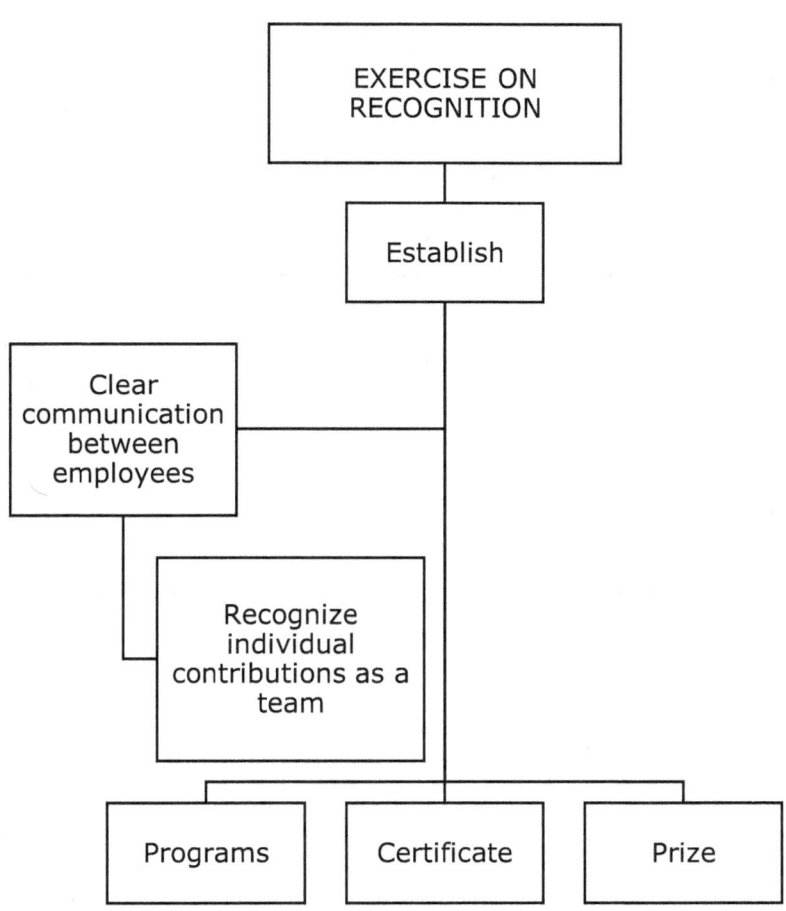

Your Mind Map No. 13

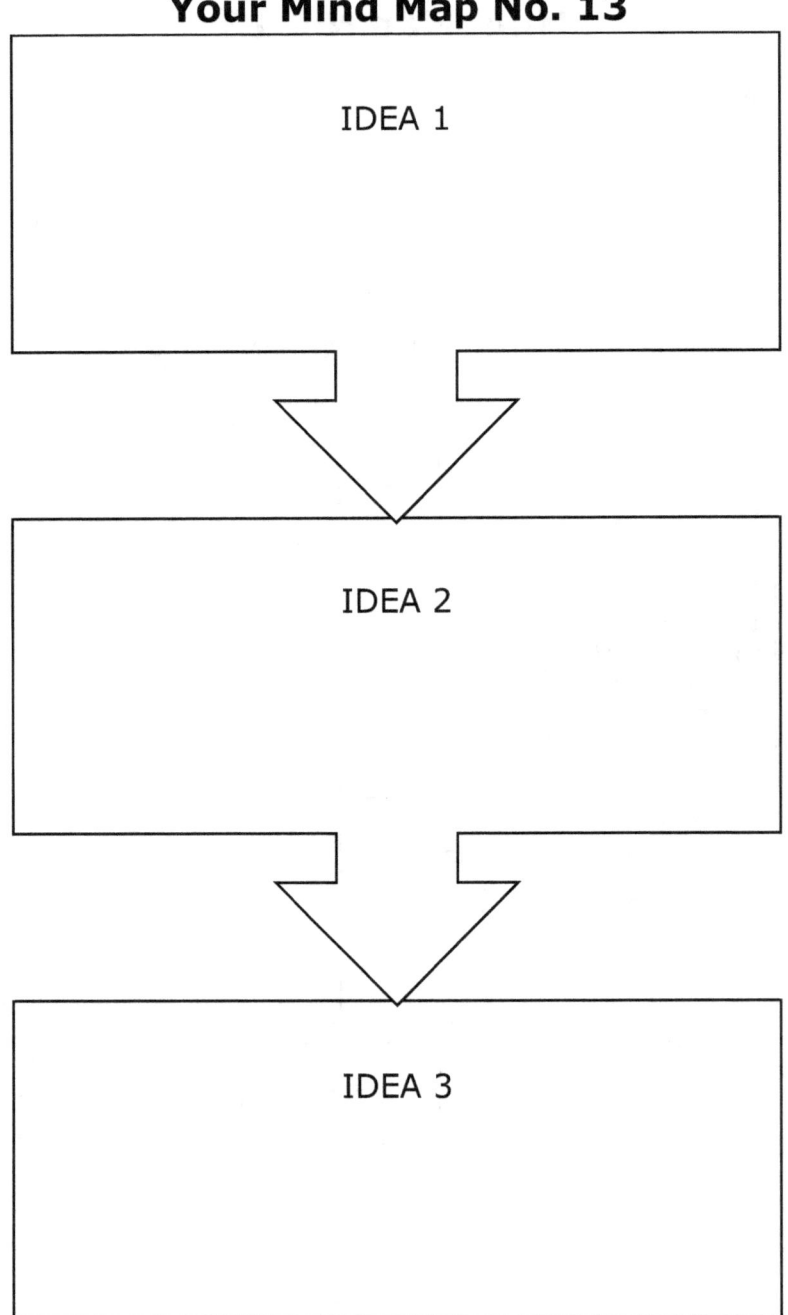

CHAPTER XIV

Performance Reward Exercise

Have you done exercises to strengthen your performance?

- ✓ An exercise to reward exceptional performance could be to offer bonuses for goals achieved.
- ✓ For example, you could establish a bonus system for employees who exceed their individual goals or team goals, and that are based on clear and objective criteria.
- ✓ An incentive program could also be offered for employees who come up with innovative ideas or creative solutions to the company's problems.
- ✓ For the program to be effective, it is important to ensure that goals and objectives are realistic and achievable, and that rewards are fair and meaningful to employees.

***

Mind Map No. 14

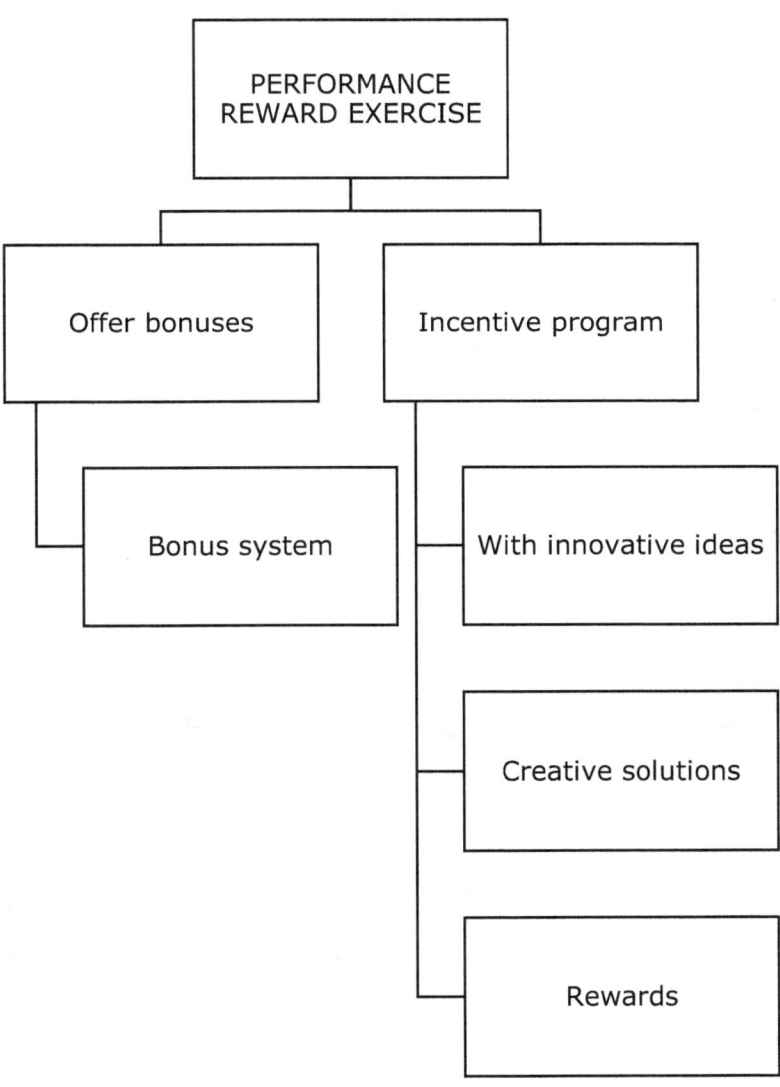

Your Mind Map No. 1 4

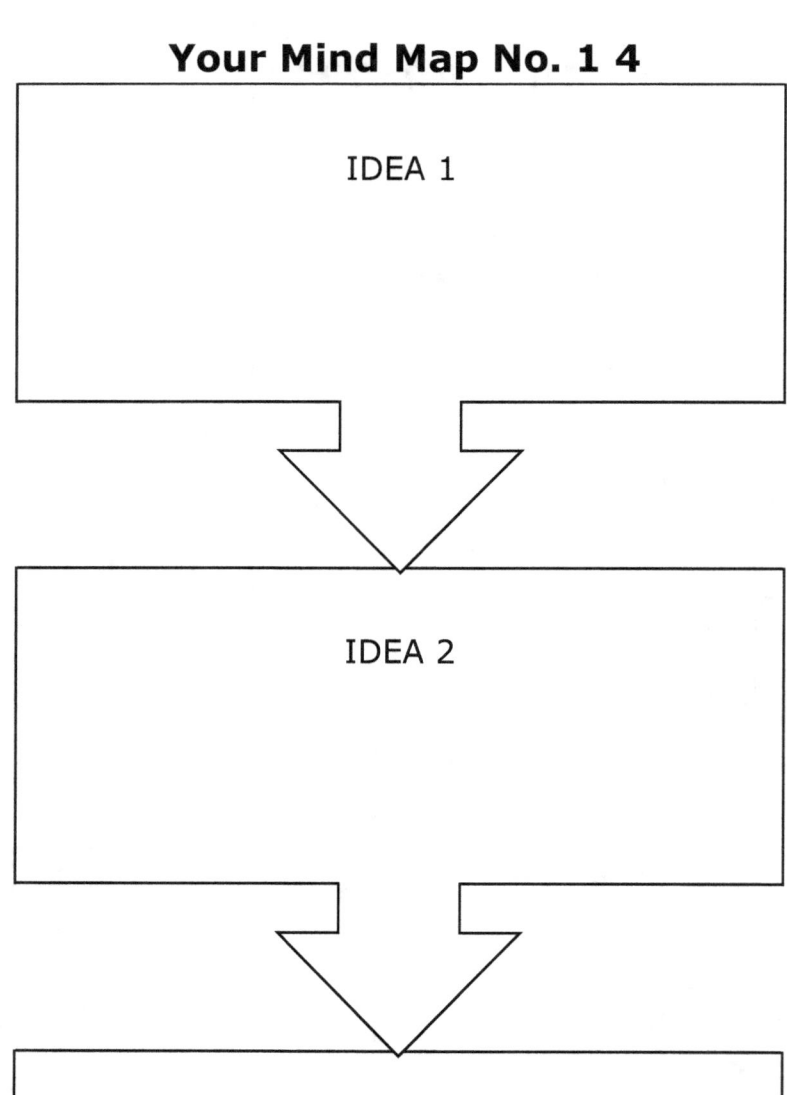

CHAPTER XV
Effective Talent Management Strategies

What would be effective strategies for human talent management?

1. Identify and attract talent.

Identify what skills and competencies are necessary for the company and attract the best talents who have those skills.

2. Develop talent.

Provide opportunities for professional and personal development, such as training, mentoring, and challenging projects.

3. Retain talent.

Offer an attractive work environment, benefits, opportunities for growth and development, recognition and fair compensation.

4. Promote diversity and inclusion.

Create an inclusive environment that values and respects employees' individual differences.

5. Evaluate performance.

Conduct regular assessments to identify talent strengths and weaknesses, and provide constructive feedback.

6. Plan succession.

Identify employees with potential for future leadership positions and provide them with opportunities to develop in that direction.

7. Promote a culture of continuous learning.

Promote a culture of continuous learning throughout the organization, where constant personal and professional development is valued.

***

Mind Map No. 15

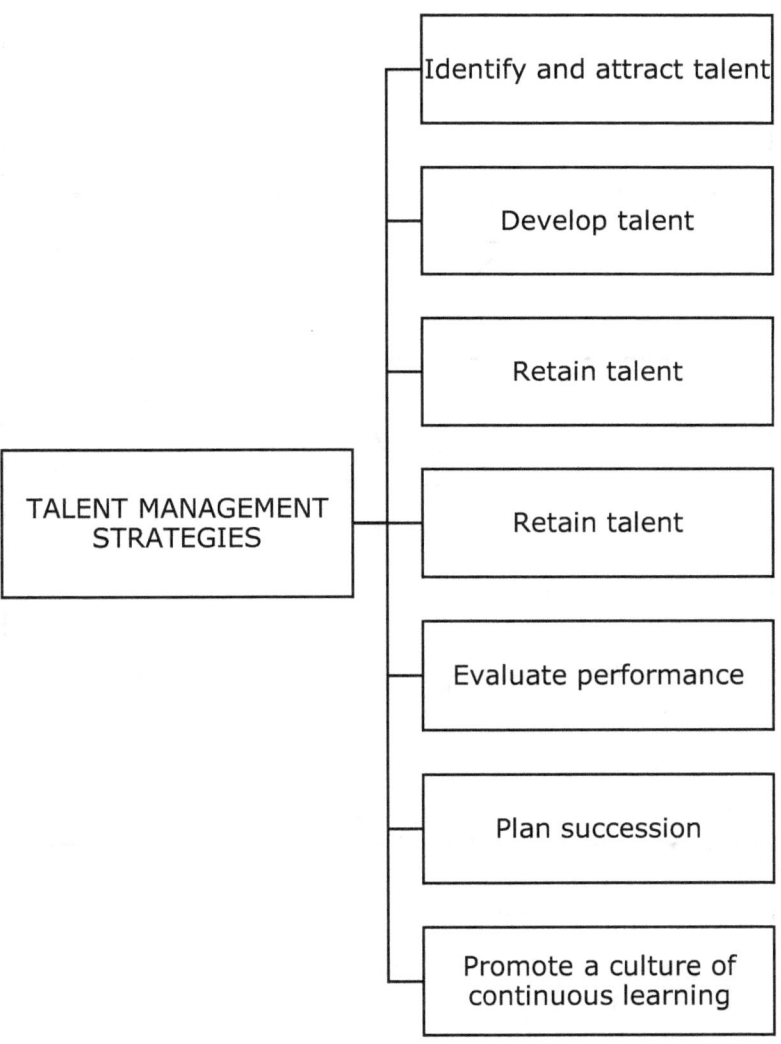

Your Mind Map No. 15

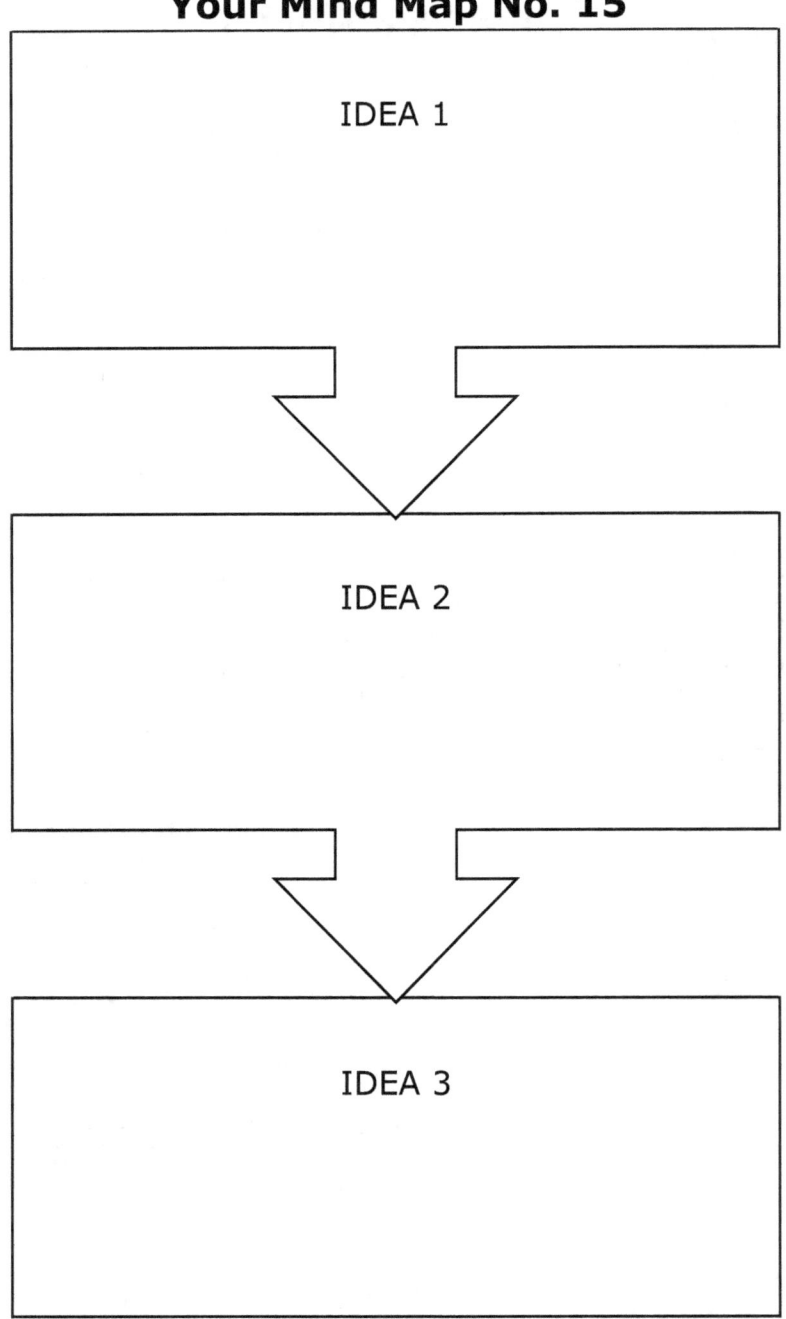

IDEA 1

IDEA 2

IDEA 3

CHAPTER XVI

Effective Strategies to Attract the Best Employees

Have you ever used strategies in your work to attract the best employees?

1. Offer an attractive work environment.

Create a pleasant, safe and comfortable work environment, with good facilities and up-to-date technology.

2. Provide opportunities for growth and development.

Offer training, mentoring, challenging projects, and opportunities for professional and personal growth.

3. Provide attractive benefits.

Offer a competitive benefits package that includes health insurance, paid vacations, days off, among others.

4. Promote company culture.

Clearly communicate company values and culture, and ensure current employees are happy and engaged with the company.

5. Use social networks.

Use social media to promote the company and its values, post job openings, and connect with potential candidates.

6. Collaborate with universities and educational institutions.

Establish relationships with universities and educational institutions to identify and attract young talent.

7. Offer fair compensation.

Offer fair compensation compared to the current job market.

***

Mind Map No. 16

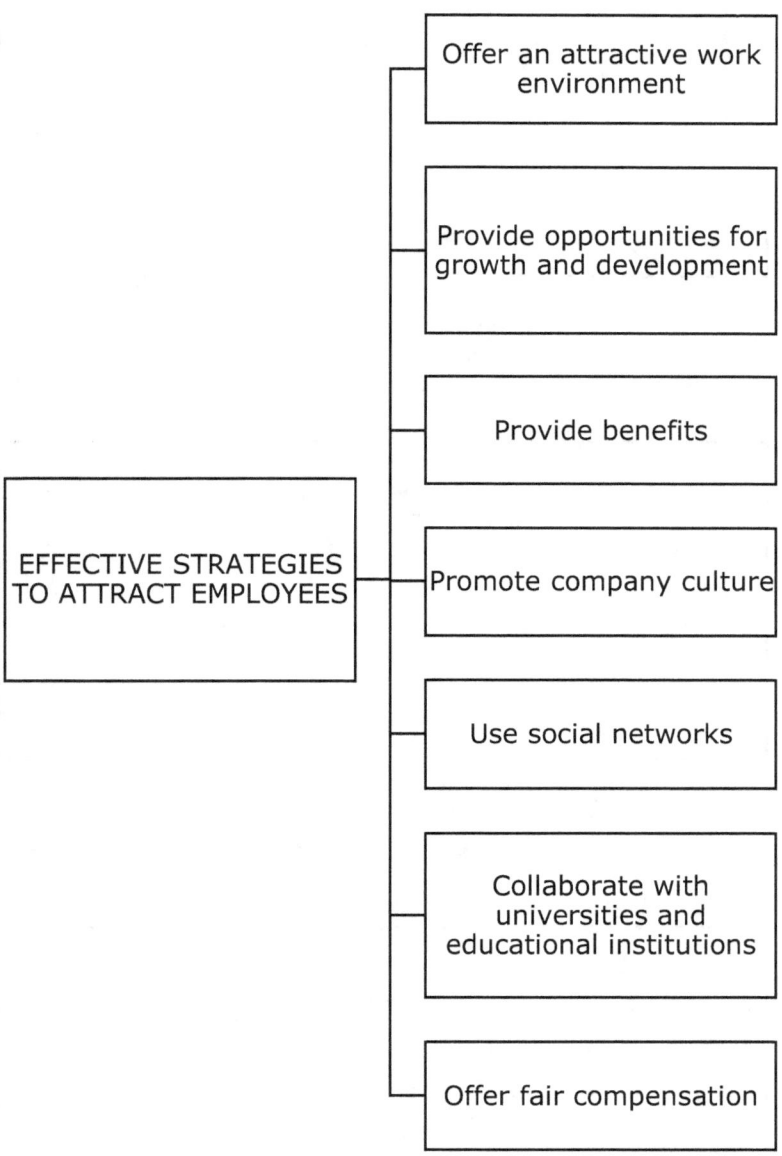

EFFECTIVE STRATEGIES TO ATTRACT EMPLOYEES

- Offer an attractive work environment
- Provide opportunities for growth and development
- Provide benefits
- Promote company culture
- Use social networks
- Collaborate with universities and educational institutions
- Offer fair compensation

Your Mind Map No. 16

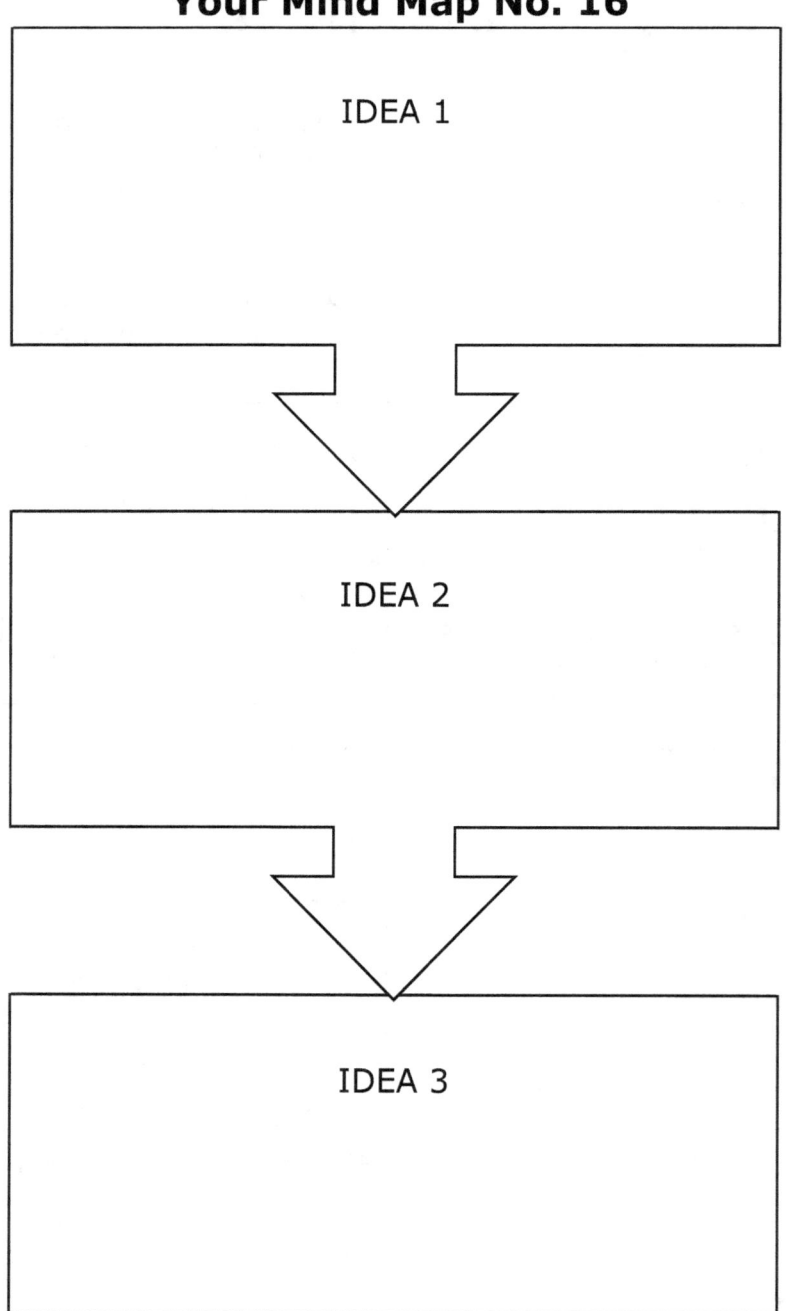

CHAPTER XVII
Strategies to Retain the Best Employees

What strategies do you know to retain the best employees?

1. Provide a positive work environment.

Create a pleasant, safe and comfortable work environment, with good facilities and up-to-date technology.

2. Offer opportunities for growth and development.

Offer training, mentoring, challenging projects, and opportunities for professional and personal growth.

3. Provide attractive benefits.

Offer a competitive benefits package that includes health insurance, paid vacations, days off, among others.

4. Promote company culture.

Clearly communicate company values and culture, and ensure current employees are happy and engaged with the company.

5. Provide constructive feedback.

Provide regular feedback on performance and areas for improvement, and recognize achievements and successes.

6. Offer fair compensation.

Offer fair compensation compared to the current job market.

7. Promote balance between personal and professional life.

Provide flexibility in work hours and allow working from home when possible, to help employees balance their personal and professional lives.

8. Recognize and reward outstanding performance.

Publicly recognize outstanding employee achievements and reward them appropriately.

***

Mind Map No. 17

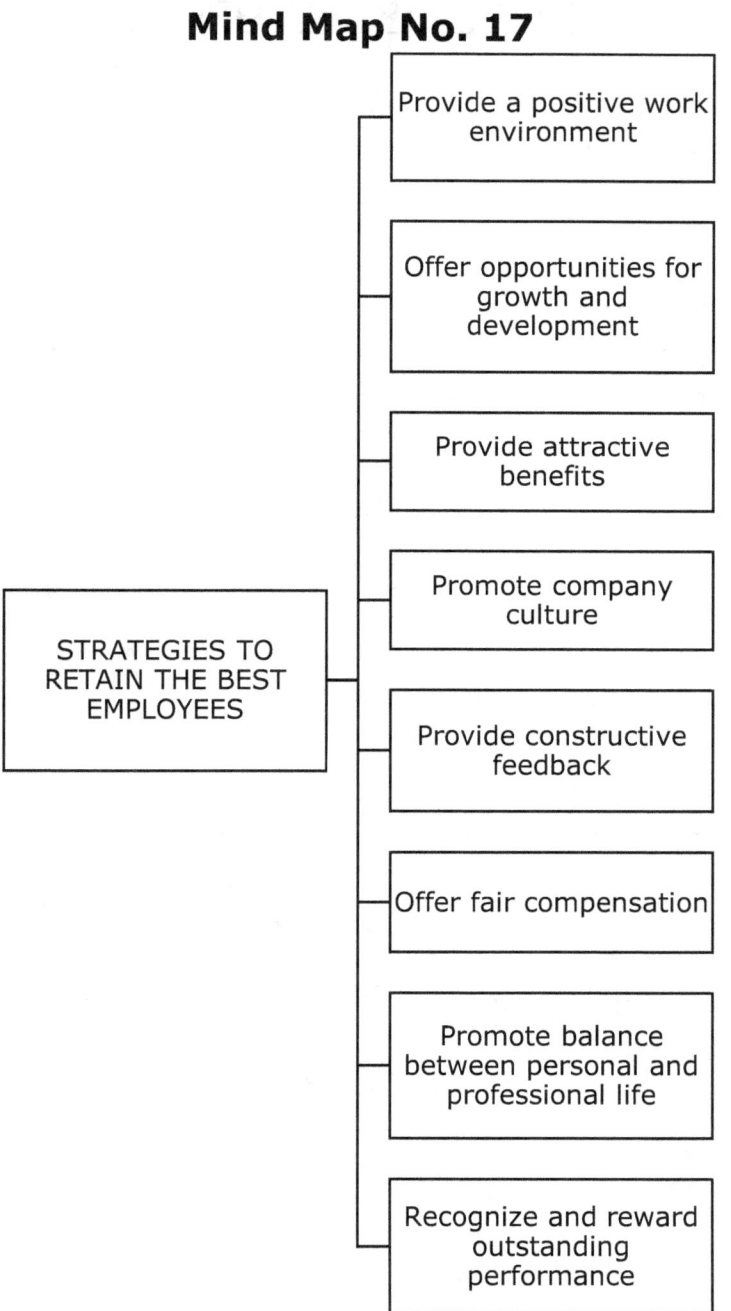

STRATEGIES TO RETAIN THE BEST EMPLOYEES

- Provide a positive work environment
- Offer opportunities for growth and development
- Provide attractive benefits
- Promote company culture
- Provide constructive feedback
- Offer fair compensation
- Promote balance between personal and professional life
- Recognize and reward outstanding performance

Your Mind Map No. 17

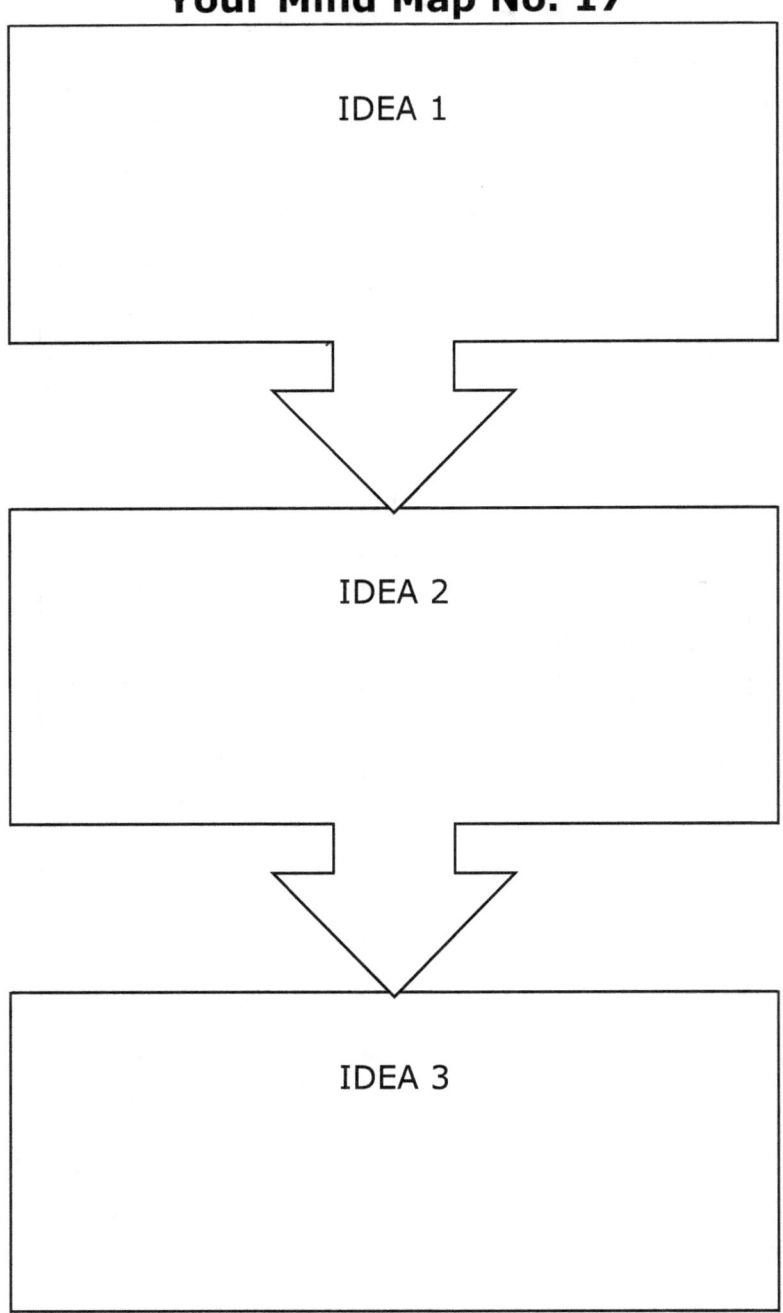

IDEA 1

IDEA 2

IDEA 3

CHAPTER XVIII
Strategies to Develop the Best Employees

What strategies do you know to develop the best human talent?

1. Provide training and development opportunities.

Offer training and development programs that help employees improve their skills and competencies.

2. Provide mentoring and tutoring.

Assign experienced mentors or tutors to help employees develop professionally.

3. Offer challenging projects.

Provide challenging projects and additional responsibilities that help employees develop new skills and competencies.

4. Provide constructive feedback.

Provide regular feedback on performance and areas for improvement, and recognize achievements and successes.

5. Offer opportunities for professional growth.

Provide opportunities for professional growth, such as internal promotions, job rotations, among others.

6. Encourage continuous learning.

Promote a culture of continuous learning throughout the organization, where constant personal and professional development is valued.

7. Provide adequate resources.

Provide necessary resources, such as updated technology, appropriate work tools, etc., to help employees perform their jobs effectively.

***

Mind Map No. 18

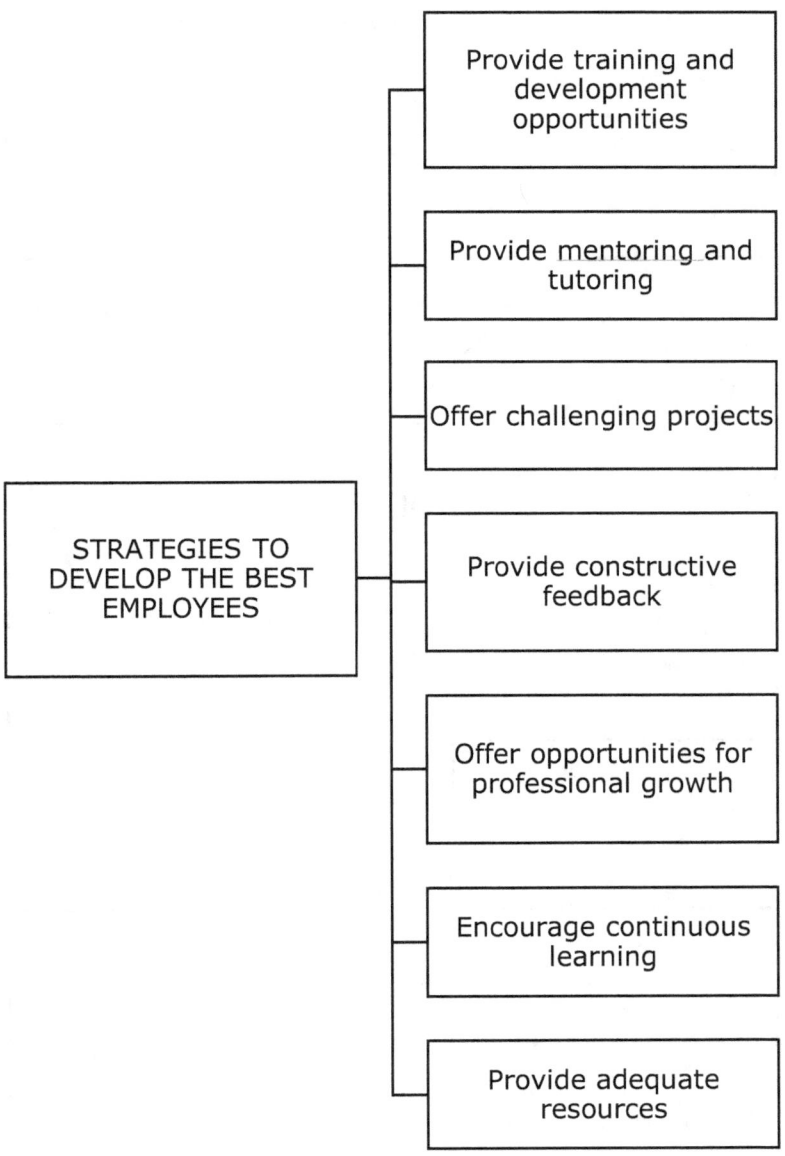

STRATEGIES TO DEVELOP THE BEST EMPLOYEES

- Provide training and development opportunities
- Provide mentoring and tutoring
- Offer challenging projects
- Provide constructive feedback
- Offer opportunities for professional growth
- Encourage continuous learning
- Provide adequate resources

Your Mind Map No. 18

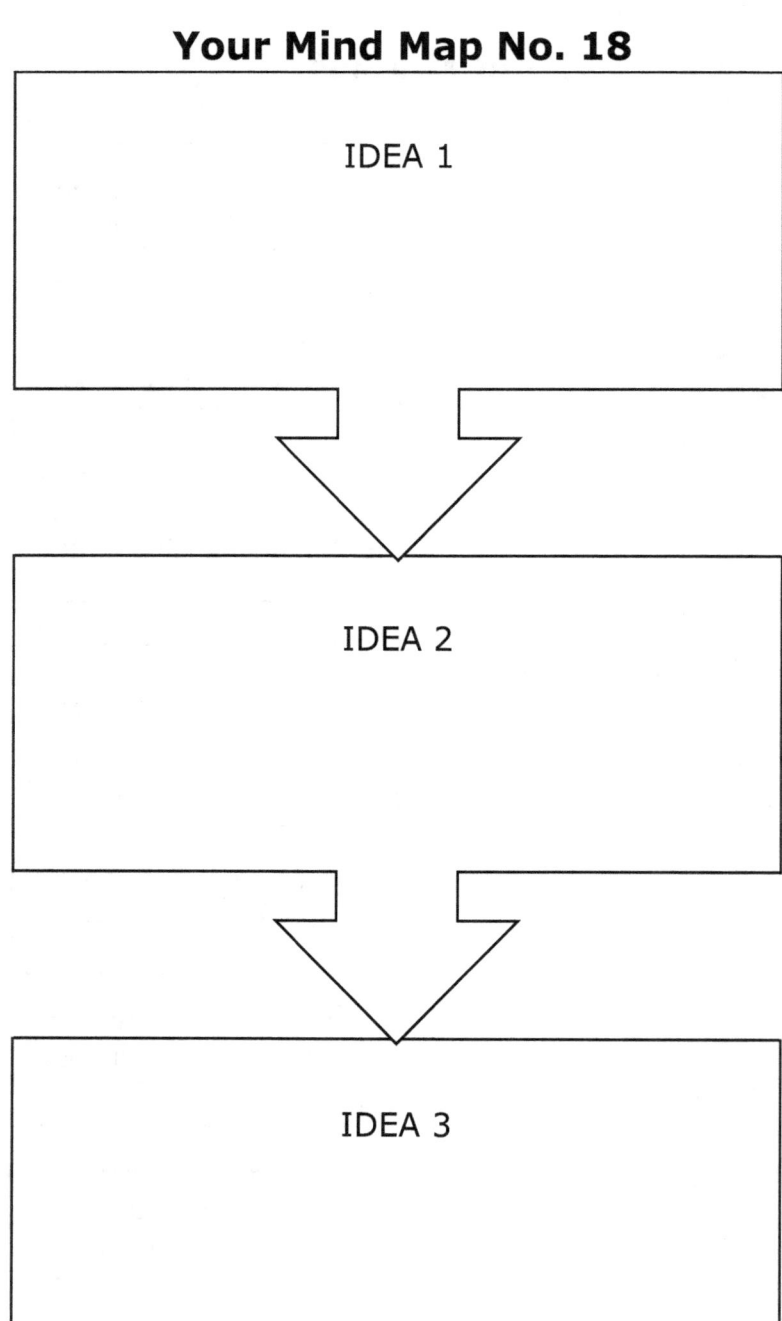

CHAPTER XIX
AI Impact Areas

Artificial intelligence (AI) is transforming the way organizations manage their human resources, from selection and hiring to talent development and retention.

*What impact do you think
artificial intelligence has
had on your work?*

Below are some areas of impact and benefits that AI brings to human resources:

1. Selection and hiring.

AI can process large amounts of data and analyze patterns to select the best candidate for a job. Instead of relying on resumes or interviews, AI can evaluate work history and look for specific skills in candidates.

2. Training and development.

AI can help identify employees' strengths and weaknesses and offer suggestions on how to improve and develop their skills by analyzing performance data, skills assessments and feedback.

3. Performance evaluation.

AI can evaluate employee performance in real time, providing constant feedback and helping managers identify opportunities for improvement in specific areas.

4. Task automation.

AI can automate HR tasks and processes such as payroll and benefits management, freeing up HR staff time to focus on more strategic tasks.

5. Improved employee experience.

AI can help improve the employee experience by personalizing the training and development experience, maximizing work-life balance, and tracking employee well-being.

However, there are also challenges that AI poses in human resource management. The automation of tasks and processes can lead to a reduction in the need for staff, which can cause concern among workers. Additionally, there are concerns that AI could lose the human factor in decision-making, especially in areas such as candidate selection or performance evaluation.

AI is transforming human resource management by delivering improved efficiency, a higher level of personalization, and consistent, accurate feedback. However, it is important to address challenges and concerns to ensure that technology supports and complements human work effectively and ethically.

***

Mind Map No. 19

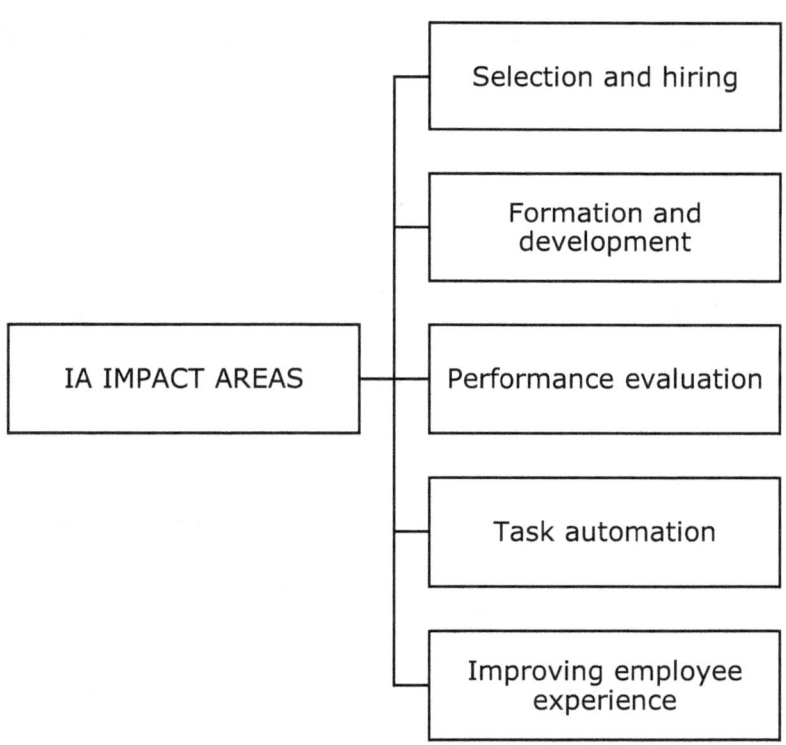

Your Mind Map No. 19

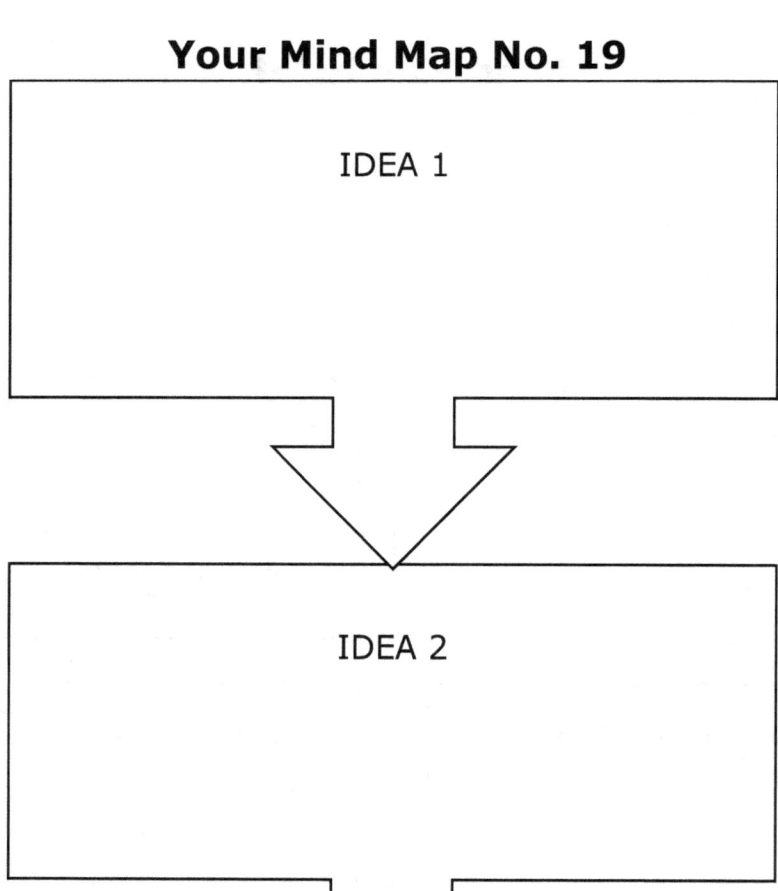

IDEA 1

IDEA 2

IDEA 3

CHAPTER XX
AI Tools

Artificial intelligence can have a major impact on human resources by automating administrative and recruiting tasks, which can save time and reduce errors.

It can also help identify patterns in employee data to improve performance and job satisfaction. However, it is also important to consider the impact on jobs and the need to retrain and relocate employees affected by automation.

How complicated do you think AI tools are for human talent management?

There are various artificial intelligence tools that can be applied in human resources management, among them are:

1. Data analysis tools.

AI can process large amounts of data related to work performance, such as survey results, assessments and training, in order to identify patterns, trends and opportunities for improvement.

2. Chatbots:

They can be used in human resources management to answer frequently asked questions from employees about company policies, benefits and vacations, among other topics. Chatbots can interact with employees quickly and efficiently, freeing up HR staff time for more strategic tasks.

3. Hiring systems with AI.

AI recruiting systems can be used to select more suitable candidates for a specific position. These systems evaluate resumes, letters of recommendation, and other information relevant to the selection process, helping to improve the quality of the process and reduce human bias.

4. Personalized training platforms.

Personalized training platforms can be used to provide personalized content to each employee based on their specific strengths, weaknesses, and training needs. These platforms can help increase employee productivity and engagement.

5. Sentiment analysis.

Sentiment analysis tools can be used to assess the emotional well-being of employees by monitoring interactions on corporate social networks and detecting early signs of discontent or dissatisfaction.

Artificial intelligence tools in human resources allow for greater efficiency in data processing, personalization and understanding of employee well-being, which contributes to more successful and effective management.

***

Mind Map No. 20

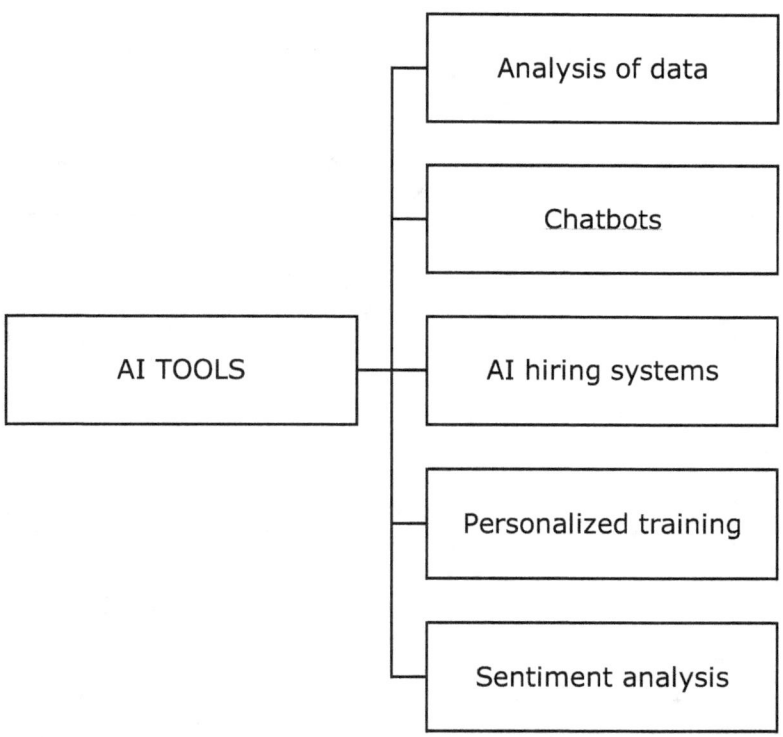

Your Mind Map No. 20

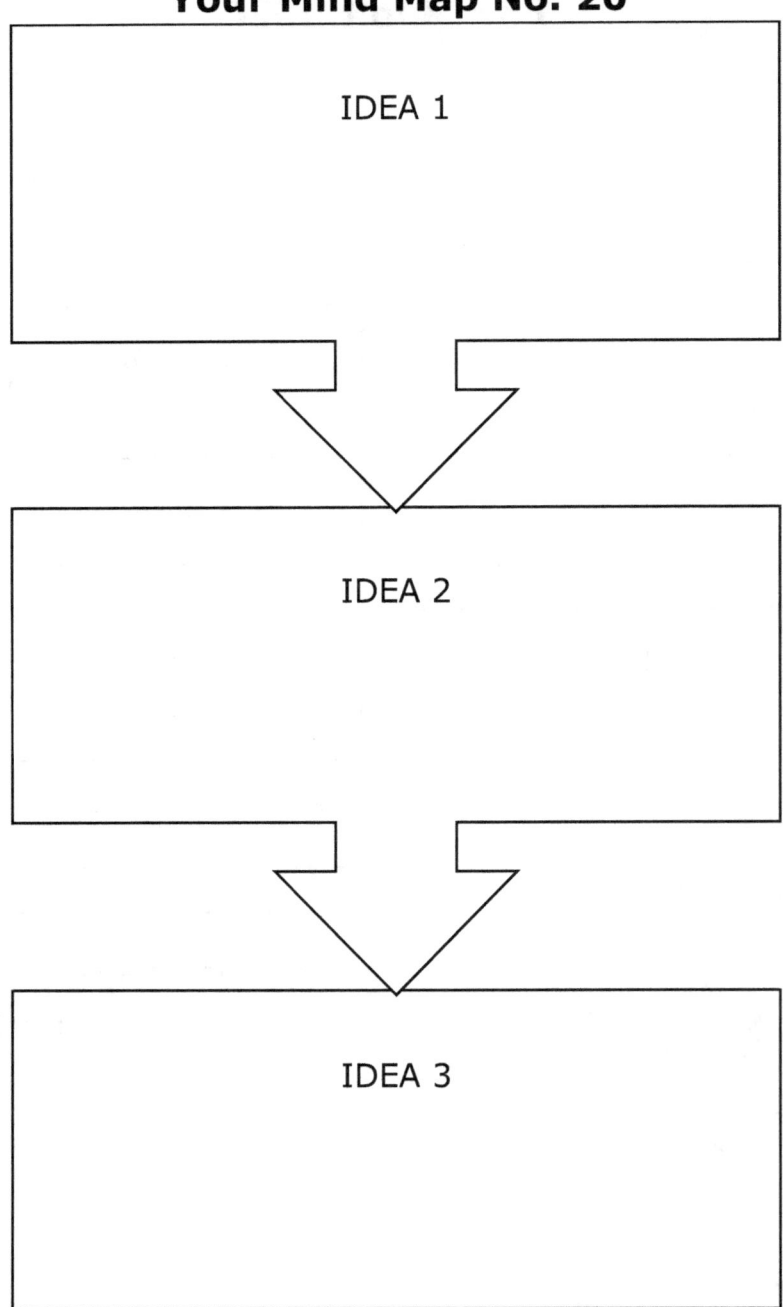

IDEA 1

IDEA 2

IDEA 3

Chapter XXI
I'm going to give you a challenge

Post a video of everything you learned in this book on your social networks and tag me #MarbellaMoyaOchoa

So that together we can share time beyond the book.

***

Mind Map No. 21

I'M GOING TO GIVE YOU A CHALLENGE

Share time beyond this book

Your Mind Map No. 21

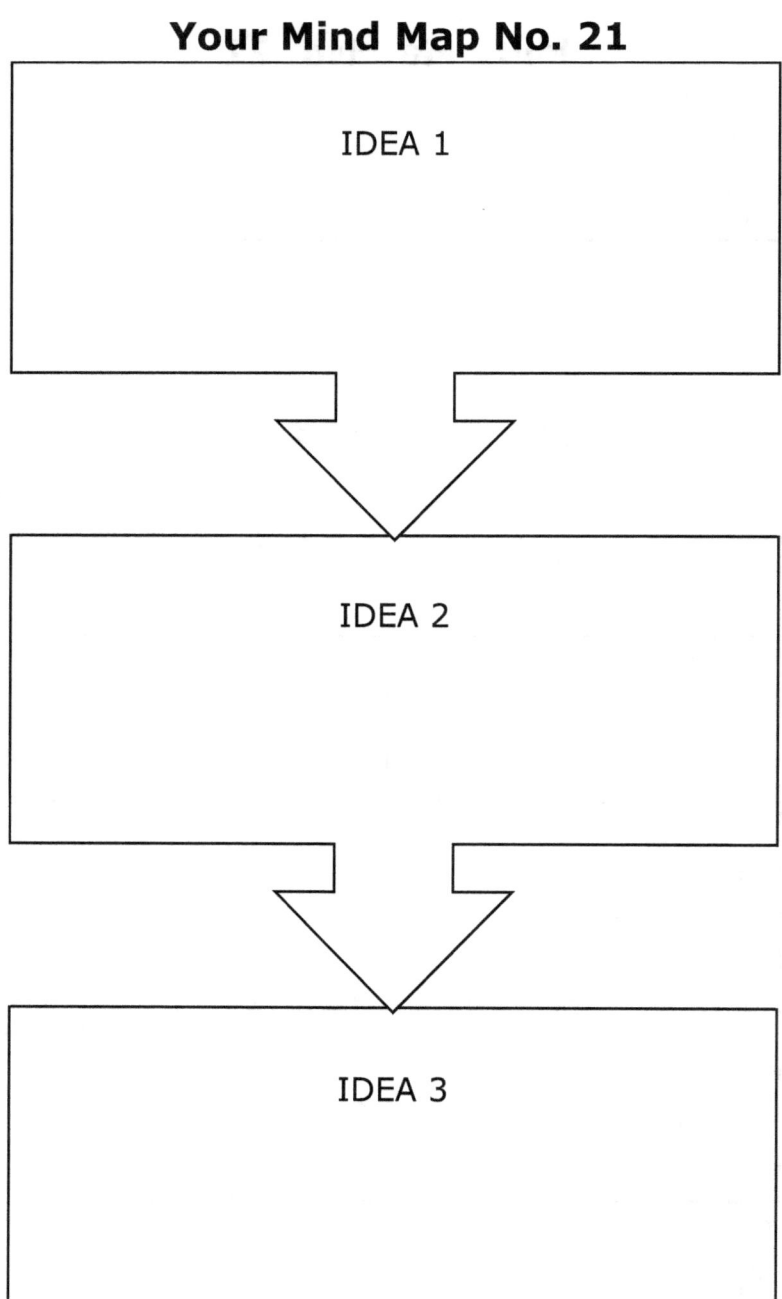

REFLECTIONS OF THE AUTHOR

In the digital age, human talent management faces new challenges and opportunities that require constant adaptation and evolution. Some of the most relevant conclusions about human talent management in the digital age are:

1. Technology should be used to improve the employee experience.

Instead of replacing human labor, technology should be used to enhance the employee experience, increase employee productivity, and improve job satisfaction.

2. Flexibility and mobility are essential.

The digital age allows us to work from anywhere and at any time, which has led to the need to offer greater flexibility and mobility to employees.

3. Continuous learning and development are essential.

Technology has also allowed greater accessibility to learning and continuous development, which has placed lifelong learning as a constant need for the development of human talent.

4. Diversity and inclusion are key.

The digital age has opened up new opportunities for diversity and inclusion in the workplace, resulting in greater creativity, innovation and problem-solving.

5. Remote management must be effective.

Managing remote teams has become common practice in the digital age, leading to the need to develop effective strategies for communication, leadership, and virtual teamwork.

In summary, human talent management in the digital era should focus on the use of technology to improve the employee experience, flexibility and mobility, continuous learning and development, diversity and inclusion, and remote management effective.

***

WORK NOTEBOOK

The workbook below contains three parts of main and supporting ideas that you will need to complete. It is also gridded to stimulate imagination and creativity, use it with total freedom and thus you will strengthen your work well-being.

Main idea 1

Secondary idea 1

Main idea 2

Secondary idea 2

Main idea 3

Secondary idea 3

READER'S REFLECTIONS

Reader's Reflections is an innovation so that the person can reason what they have read and put it into practice.

From a series of questions about the entire content of the book, the reader can respond according to his or her own criteria, making the reading go beyond the traditional because learning is reinforced and places the reader as an active participant in each written word, generating a inseparable interaction between writer and reader.

This relationship is dynamism, to the extent that reading is greatly reinforced and motivates us to transform our world from the static to the mobile, because the reading of any book is the movement of ideas and ultimately the reader's reflections complement people's intellect.

According to what you read, what do human talent strategies in the digital age mean to you?

_____

_____

_____

_____

_____

_____

_____

_____

_____

How do you apply what you learned in society?

How do you think these strategies apply
on the world stage?

_____

_____

_____

_____

_____

_____

_____

_____

_____

_____

How would what you learned in this book be applied in your work area?

What changes in Human Resources
Management learning and work practices
should exist today?

_____

_____

_____

_____

_____

_____

_____

_____

_____

INTELLECTUAL AUTOBIOGRAPHY

WRITER
POLITHOLOGIST
ADMINISTRATOR

I was born in the city of Caracas in Venezuela. Professional in Political Science and Administration with more than 13 years of experience. Human Rights Specialist.

I am a multifaceted woman as a writer, Political Scientist and Administrator, inveterate Entrepreneur and Human Resources Mentor by conviction.

Graduated in 2010 with a degree in Political and Administrative Sciences from the Central University of Venezuela, with a mention in Political Science. Simultaneously, I obtained a Bachelor's degree in Administration with a mention in Material and Financial Resources from the Simón Rodríguez National Experimental University. In both within the top 10 of the promotion.

Since 2018, I have assumed the commitment to be CEO – President of the Educando Para La Paz FEPAZ WORLD Foundation, promoting a culture of peace in the human rights of children and families that builds fraternal coexistence without exclusion.

In the same year, she ventured as a freelance writer for Amazon.com, Inc. or its affiliates.

In 2020, Amazon.com, Inc. or its subsidiaries, granted me Amazon Influencer recognition on social networks and through them I teach about the political, social and economic reality of countries, from the human perspective, focusing on working for a world better for love of childhood.

In 2022, I will promote FEPAZ World Academy to more than 100,000 students from 135 countries.

In 2023, the Human Resources Academy and Consultant – ARH International began, to promote the personal and work well-being of people in an innovative and exponential way. In the same year I started the Human Rights Academy – ADH International.

As outstanding features, I am academically trained in Politics, Administration, Economics, Statistics, Psychology, Philosophy, History, Sociology, International Relations and Law, to observe the environment in a global, critical and objective manner.

BOOKS PUBLISHED ON AMAZON.COM, INC. OR ITS AFFILIATES.

Human Resources Series

HUMAN RESOURCES
Volume I Agile Skills:
Become an expert in leadership and developing high-performance teams.

HUMAN RESOURCES
Volume II Professional Challenges:
Learn the art of leading effective teams.

HUMAN RESOURCES
Volume III Talent Management in the Digital Age:
Develop high-impact business strategies.

- ***My social networks: Marbella Moya Ochoa***
  @mymarbellaochoa

- ***Email: mymarbellaochoa@gmail.com***

- To see more of any series visit my store on Amazon:
  https://www.amazon.com/shop/mymarbellaochoa

- Author page on Amazon:
  https://www.amazon.com/author/mymarbellaochoa

The publication of this work was carried out by:

Marbella Yeniree Moya Ochoa.

Independently published on Amazon.com, Inc. or its affiliates.

This work was published on June 25, 2023.

In Caracas – Venezuela.

www.ingramcontent.com/pod-product-compliance
Lightning Source LLC
Chambersburg PA
CBHW070020300526

45794CB00001B/370